Cool Stuff Drawing

How to Draw the Best of Cool Drawings in the Easiest Way

By Derek Stewart

Copyright©2015 Derek Stewart

Table of Contents

Disclaimer

While all attempts have been made to verify the information provided in this book, the author does assume any responsibility for errors, omissions, or contrary interpretations of the subject matter contained within. **The information provided in this book is for educational and entertainment purposes only. The reader is responsible for his or her own actions and the author does not accept any responsibilities for any liabilities or damages, real or perceived, resulting from the use of this information.**

The trademarks that are used are without any consent, and the publication of the trademark is without permission or backing by the trademark owner. All trademarks and brands within this book are for clarifying purposes only and are the owned by the owners themselves, not affiliated with this document.

Introduction

Artists have different purposes behind drawing various illustrations. Some of them draw just for entertainment, while others draw for the sole satisfaction of their inner soul. There is no dearth of commercial artists as well. In fact, most of the artists these days start their career to join the mainstream artists in any way possible. But, whatever you motto behind drawing is, you must clear your basics.

In this book, we have discussed basically about pencil drawings. The book is written according to the needs of amateur artists who have just started their practice sessions with pencil. The book will teach you how you can create marvelous drawings using simple techniques and methods.

The reading section in the first part of the book explains how you can confront and deal with your wants of drawings. Sometimes, you just feel like drawing something but you do not know where to start from. This is where we come in. We will let you know how you can feed your cravings for drawing just "anything".

The book also contains a few tips on drawing with pencil or graphite. The tips will come in handy if you are completely new to try pencil. Even the experienced artists can take help from the book. The book is written to satiate all levels of artist.

Section 1
Chapter 1   Why should you draw?

This question often arises in my mind, why should I draw? What should I draw? Who can answer these questions? It's none other than me. It is a question of introspection. As an artist, you know that you can doodle on a few corners of the pages. But, does that qualify you to be an artist? Yes, it does. Anybody who wants and can draw anything on earth qualifies to be an artist. It's just that in many of us, the artist is dormant. We have to pull the drawing beast out of his quilt and just sit down to draw.

You must be wondering how that is possible. How can you just push yourself to draw? Art is meditation. If you feel that you want to relax with drawing, you can sit down to draw. If you feel that you need to vent out your frustrations, art is a perfect medium to express your feelings on paper without harming anyone. You might come across an idea sometimes which you feel that you must express or the world should know about it. At such times, you can grab a paper and a pencil and draw whatever you feel like. The outcome will definitely be something interesting.

It is interesting to know that Salvador Dali, the world famous artist used to keep a pen and a paper beside his bed when he slept. He would wake at the midnight and scribble whatever he dreamt and slept again. Then, he would get up in the morning and give life to his dreams on the canvas. Now, you can imagine that artists can go to any extent to listen to the call of the artist inside them.

What should you draw?

The logic says that you must start with copying the drawing of just anything you come across to start with. But, we say no. You must give some time to yourself to analyze what you are good at. Look around the books you have, browse internet, meet some other artists, and do whatever you can to find your forte. Once you find it, then you can start perfecting your drawings. I am not saying that you should not begin drawing till the time you do not find your muse. It's just that keep practicing with other drawings simultaneously till the time you develop you style. You can start with scribbling and then move ahead to drawing more sophisticated things later.

A style of the artist is very important to make you stand class apart among others. If you just go on copying what other are doing, you will never be able to make a name for yourself. That is why, it is very crucial for every artist to make unique paintings to maintain originality and command respect of other artists.

There are hundreds of genres of art. You can analyze some of them and specialize in any one of them. Start drawing with one genre and when you specialize in it, you can switch to another genre as well. In addition, do not stick to one genre that you had selected earlier if you find that you are not able to associate with it. Art is for soul. If you do not find satisfaction with the art you draw, you will not be able to enjoy it, which is very crucial for an artist. You can succeed only if you enjoy what you do.

One more important aspect of drawing is that you must keep patience and give yourself ample of time. Things take time in every arena to give results.

Getting started

For getting started with pencil drawings, or graphite drawings, you must have the basic equipment's. Don't worry. They are nothing fancy but just a good quality pencil and a sketch book. There are different grades of pencils within different brands even if they come with the same number. Plus, there are different textures of graphite. Some are rough and coarse in texture which gives a unique look to the drawings, which other are softer, which are also distinct for drawing.

It is also important that you practice regularly. However, for some people it is next to impossible to dedicate 4-5 hours every day with other chores of the routine. Thus, you can just take a small sized sketch book and carry it wherever you go. When you have your equipment in your bag every time, you can scribble anything you see around to practice when you have to sit idle. For example, while travelling or while waiting for your friends in a restaurant, you can take benefit of the situation.

Chapter 2 Tips for Pencil Drawing

You might be aware of pencil drawing and using raw graphite sticks for drawing and shading. However, there are some things which we skip when we are doing the art work. We have mentioned a few tips and tricks for pencil shading, which might help you in your work in future.

Making marks with pencil

Making marks with pencil means that when you touch your pencil on a piece of paper, it makes various marks on it depending upon how you use it. To learn making such marks, you should explore the various possibilities of your pencil. It is not just a drawing tool; it is a kind of magic wand in your hands with which you can make endless breathtaking designs. Explore the pencil by applying different pressure variations and also try different types of lines. You should be able to control the marks wherever needed.

Sharpen your pencils

A few techniques of drawing require blunt pencils or chisel cut pencils. Apart from those, you must keep your pencils sharp at all times. Forget about the "wasted" graphite in the sharpener. It is absolutely fine. At least it is better than wasting your efforts of drawing. Softer pencils are used for drawing darker lines. But, they go blunt quickly as well.

Use various kinds of lines

The line-weight is one very important aspect of the pencil. When you press the pencil or lift it up, the variations come in lines. Explore the possibilities. Start with less pressure and keep increasing it afterwards.

Even shading

Try to achieve even shading throughout the drawing. If there are variations within the drawing, maintain evenness in its parts wherever necessary. Uneven shading gives a messy look. Also, avoid greasing your palm and wrist with graphite from the paper. The more you touch your hands on the paper, the messier your drawing will become.

Make the marks according to the composition of the subject

You must do the shading according to the requirements of the subject. If your drawing requires smooth and gentle shading, do not force the pencil too much on the paper. If the subject requires scruffy shading, you can take a sharper pencil.

Hold the pencil properly

If you hold your pencil close to the nib, it will give you more command over the tool. However, if you hold it too close to the nib, it might obstruct the view of the drawing.

Use different techniques of shading

There are several techniques of shading. You must learn all of them to incorporate in your drawings. Some of these techniques include hatching, cross hatching, stipping, back and forth stroke, scumbling, etc.

Section 2
Chapter 1 How to draw a Victorian lamp

Step 1

We will start drawing the cool drawings with a lamp, which is inspired from the Victorian era. Draw the outline of the lamp shade. The bottom border of the lampshade is curved so that we can design frills there later. The outline we draw here is just a bunch of guiding lines. Therefore, you must draw them in a very light tone.

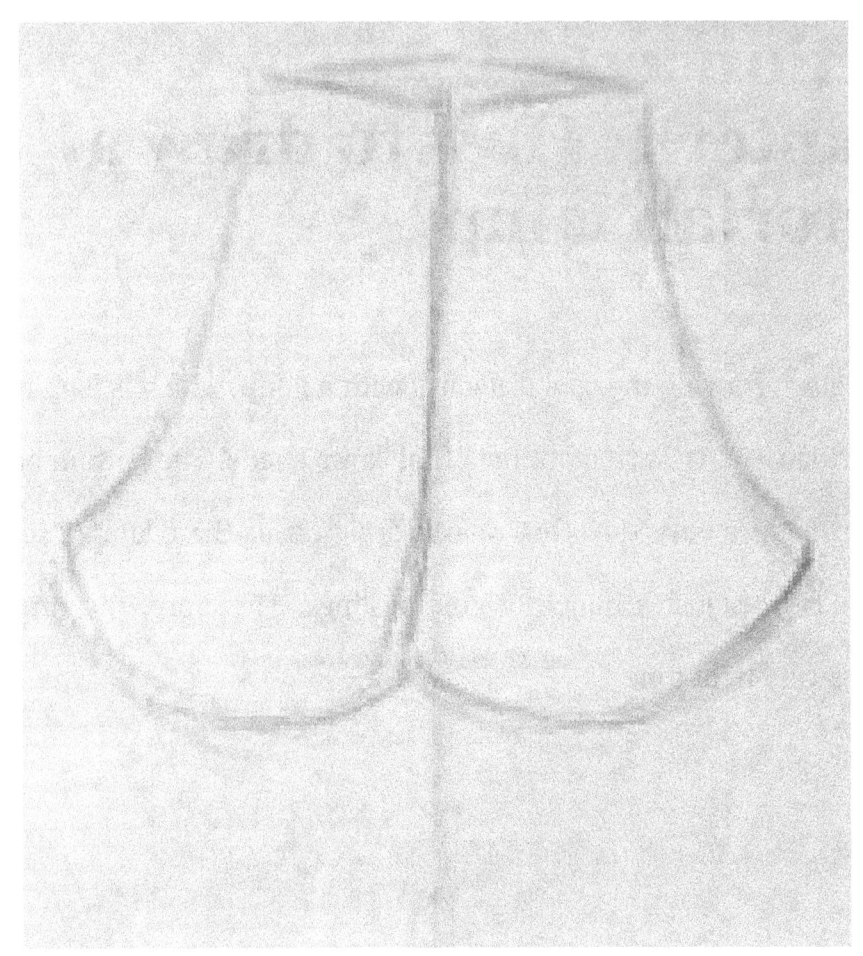

Step 2

On the upper ring of the lampshade, draw a design of frilled clothing. You can modify the illustration given here according to your choice.

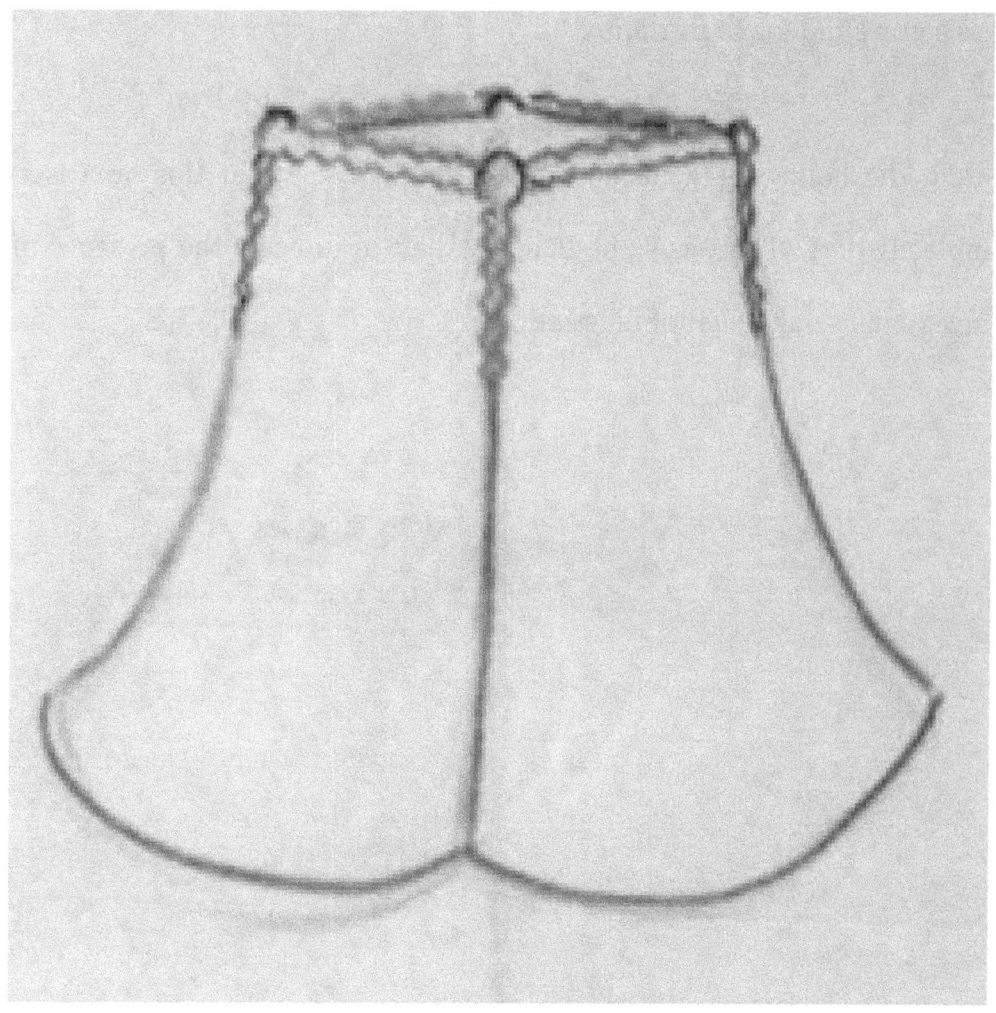

Step 3

In s similar pattern, draw a frilled embellishment on the lower ring of the lampshade. The fringes of the design should be hanging along the border. It gives a graceful look to the lamp.

Darken the hollow area inside the top ring. Notice that this area is not completely dark. There is some light part left to indicate the presence of a source of light on the left of illustration.

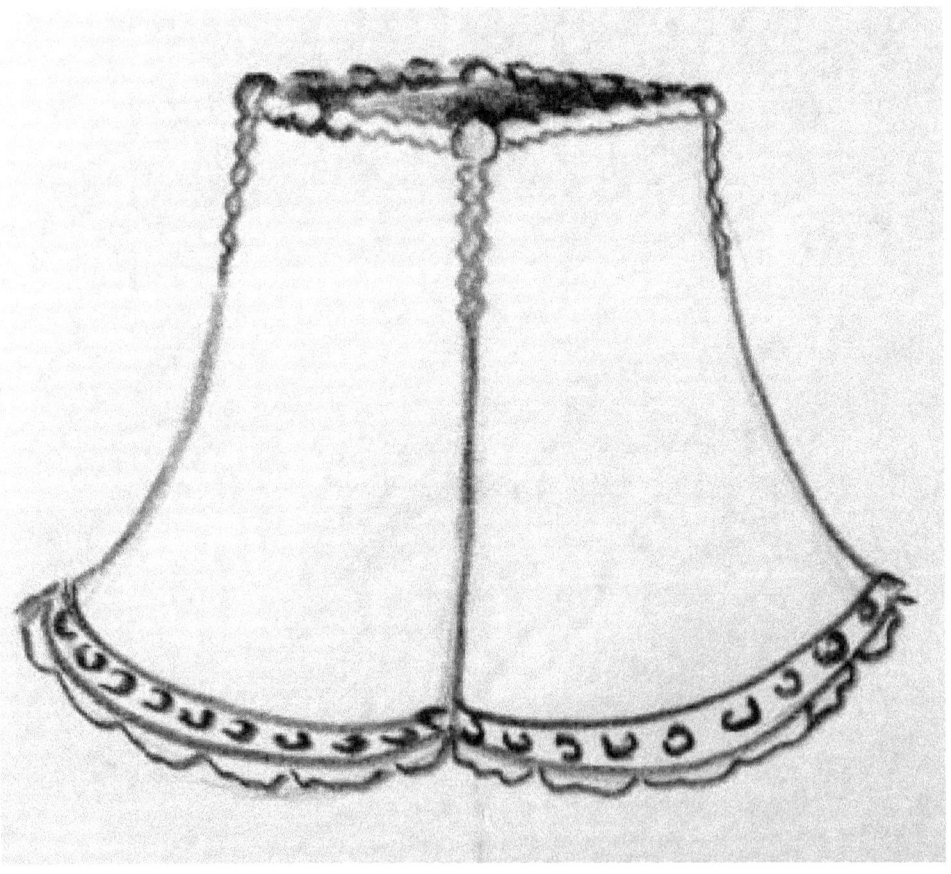

Step 4

Fill up the frills with required shading on both the borders.

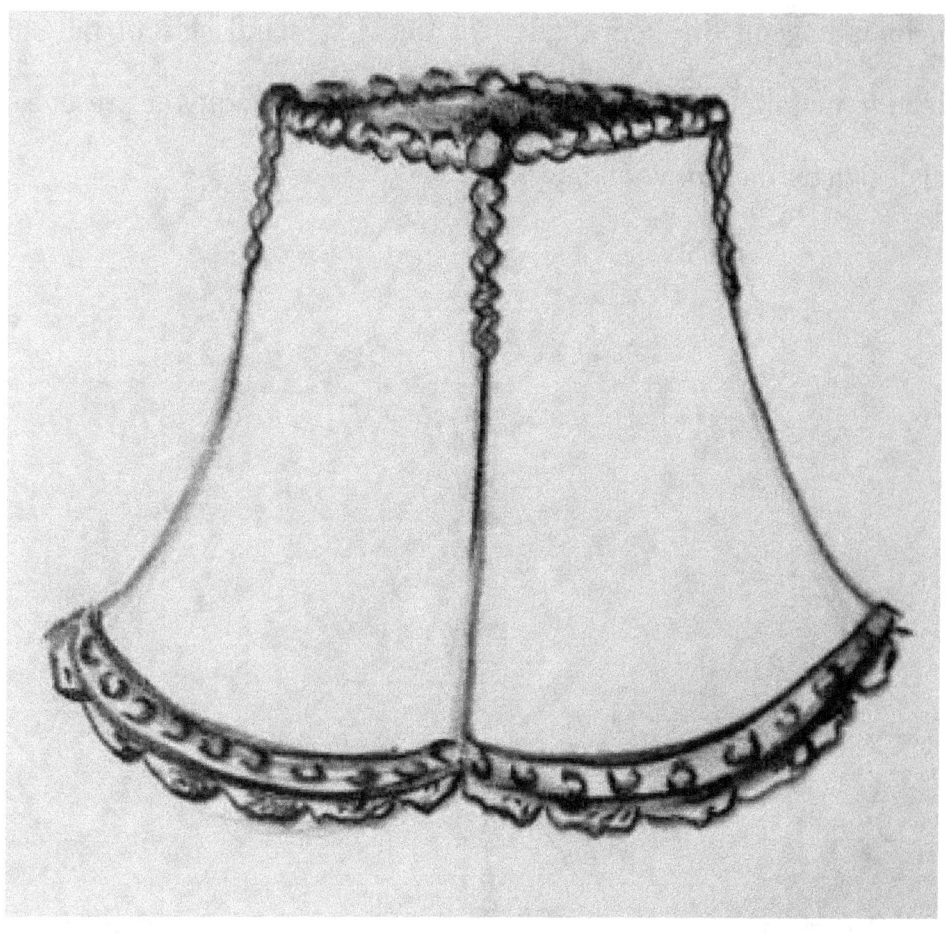

Step 5

Along the vertical piping, scribble some diagonal lines to suggest the idea of sunlight falling on the lampshade. On the right hand side of the shade, scribble some random curved lines also. These lines denote the presence of a floral design on the cloth of lampshade.

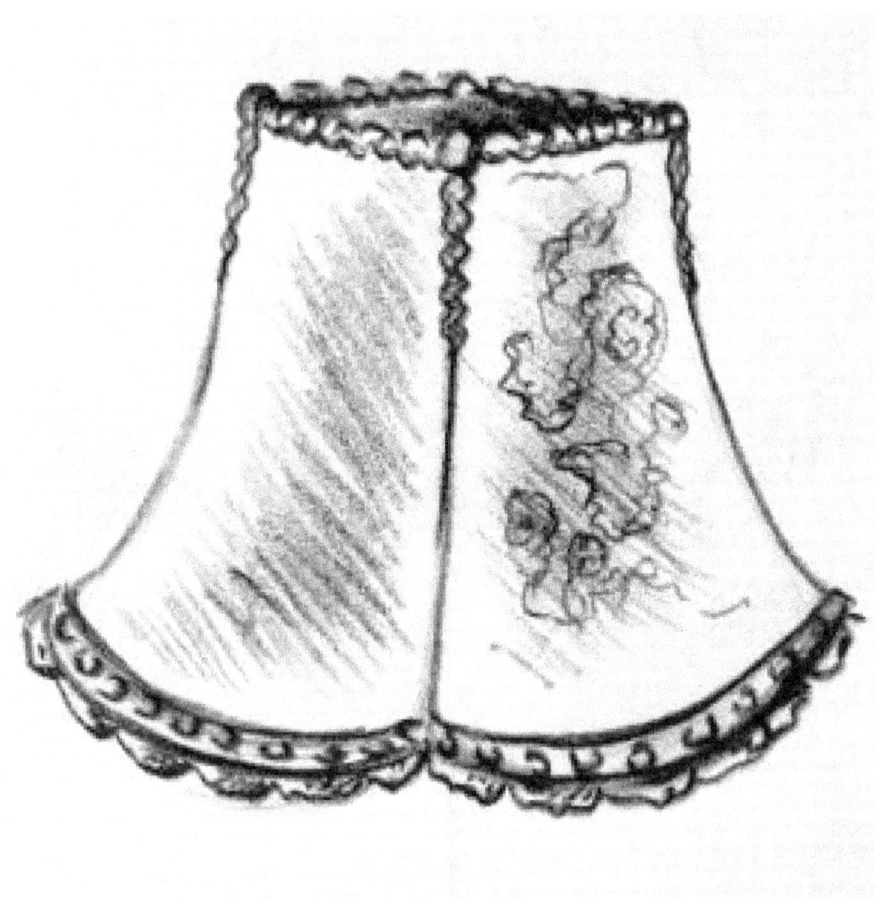

Step 6

Scribble the similar floral pattern on the left of vertical piping also overlapping the diagonal scribbles. You can also use white pencil to vary the gradation of sunlight. A white pencil is used to highlight the reflection of light beforehand.

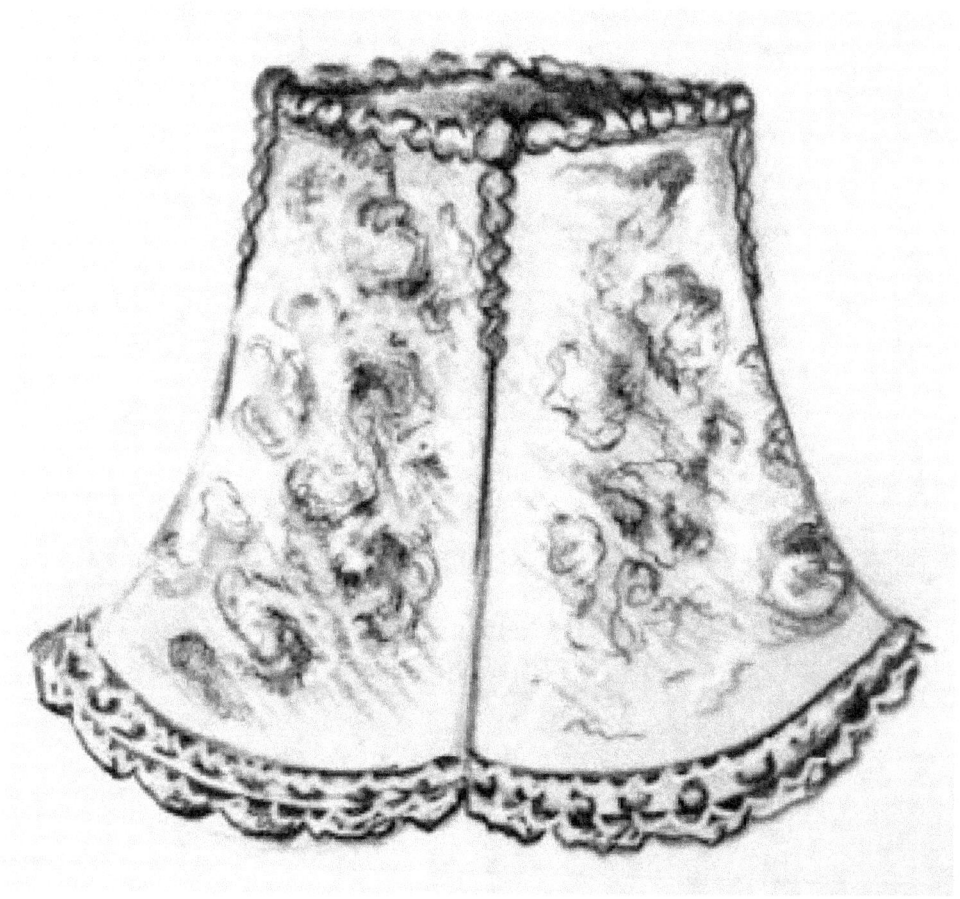

Step 7

Draw the lamp base and neck using black pencil. Maintain the delicacy of the base while drawing the outline.

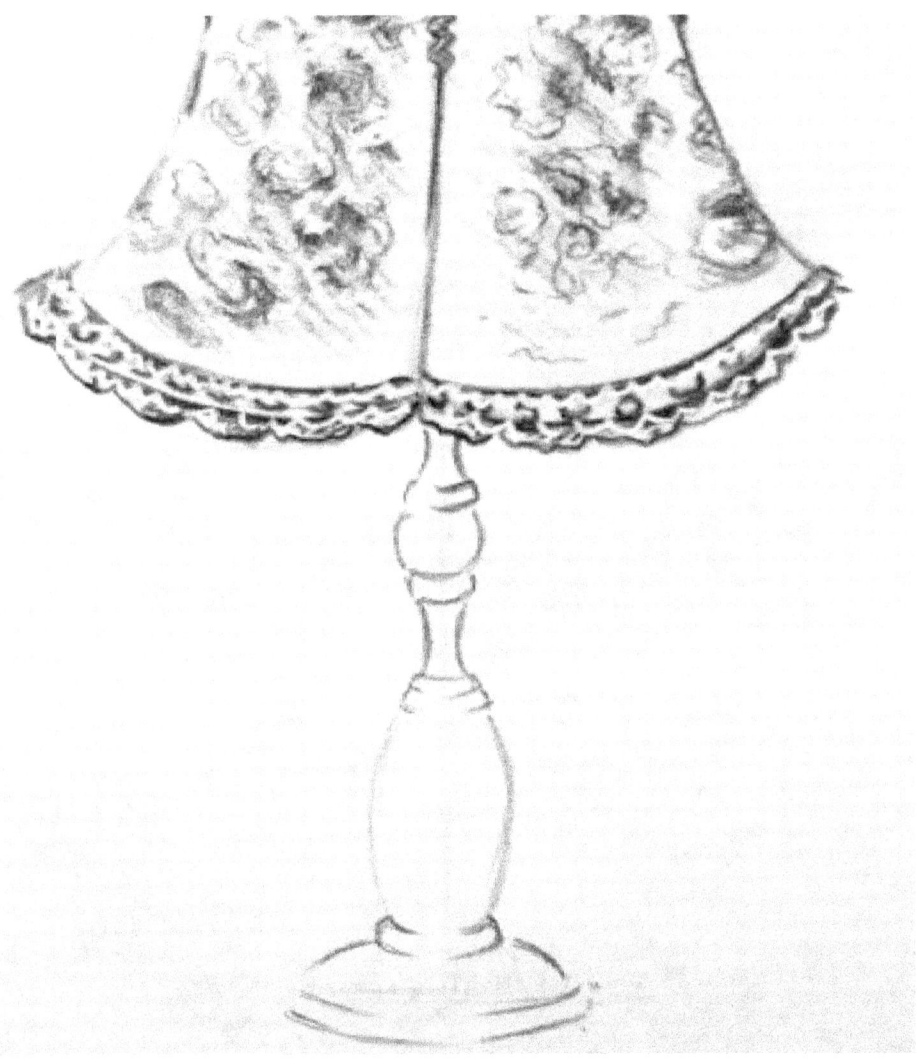

Step 8

Start shading the neck and rest of the lamp base. The source of light plays a very important role in drawing and shading. It helps us to determine how much lighter or darker should the shading be. Here, the source of light is from the left of the picture. Thus all the reflection part of the shading and white highlights should be on the left.

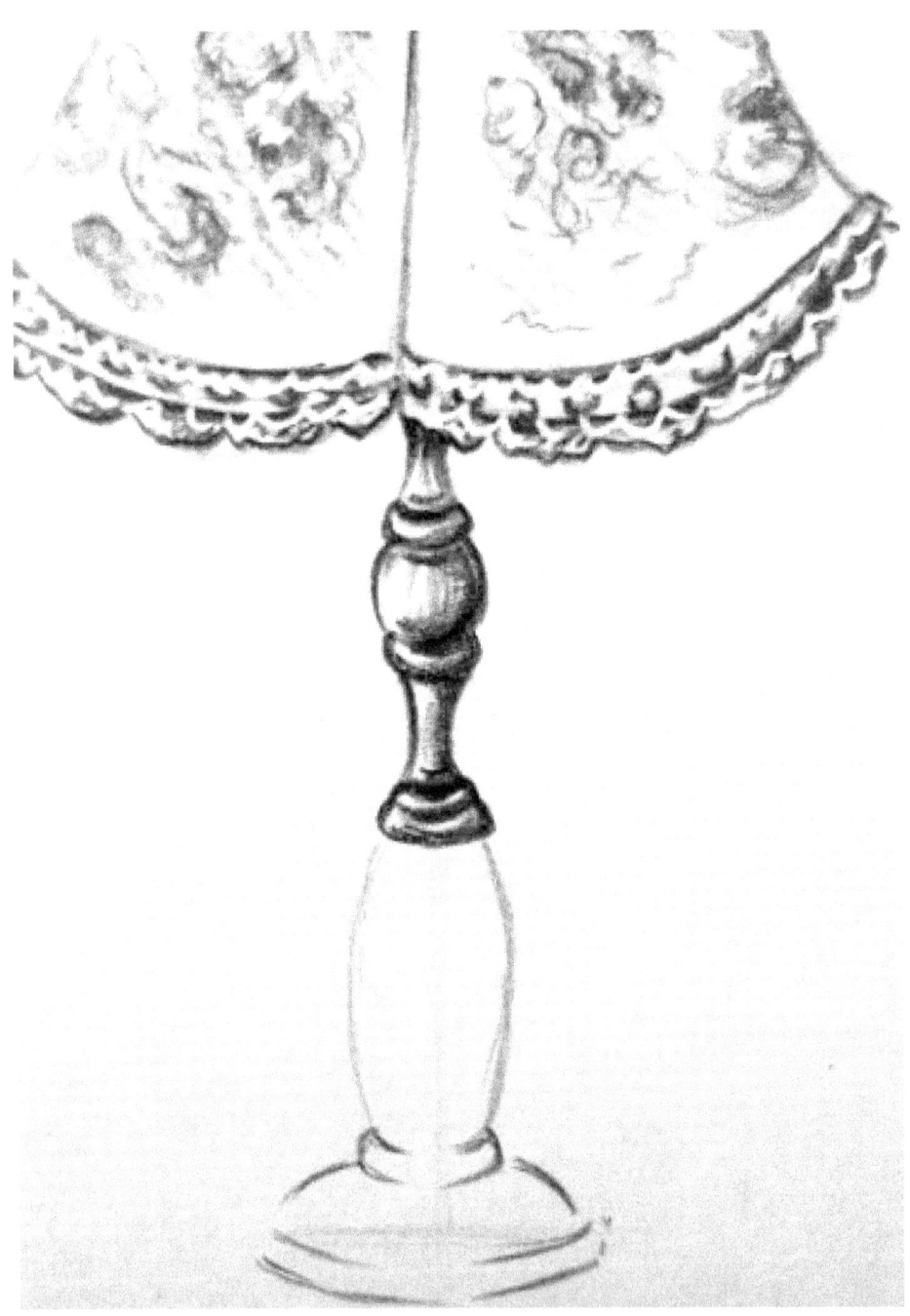

Step 9

Take a look at the close up of the base. The shading has been beautifully given to highlight the variation in light. The darkest portions of the lamp base are on the extreme right side. This denotes the absence of light or very minor presence of it.

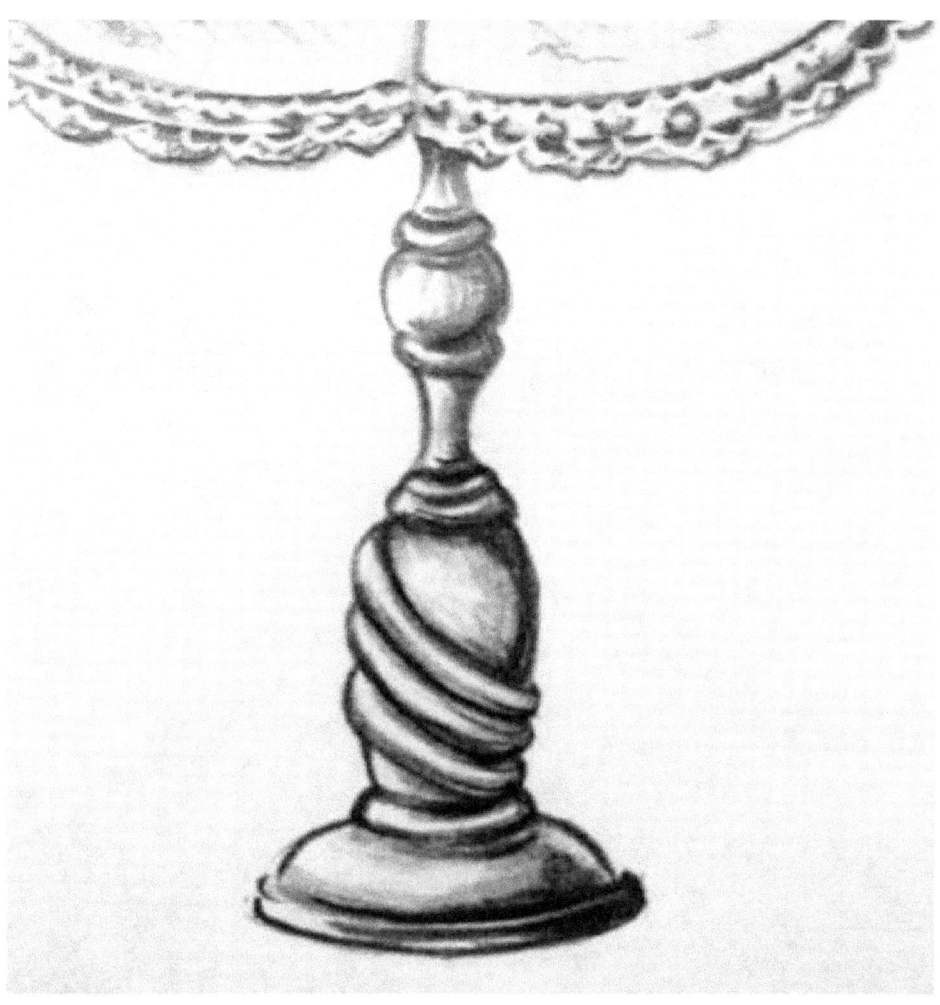

Step 10

Give finishing touches to the lamp. Darken and lighten the shading wherever necessary. The Victorian lamp is complete.

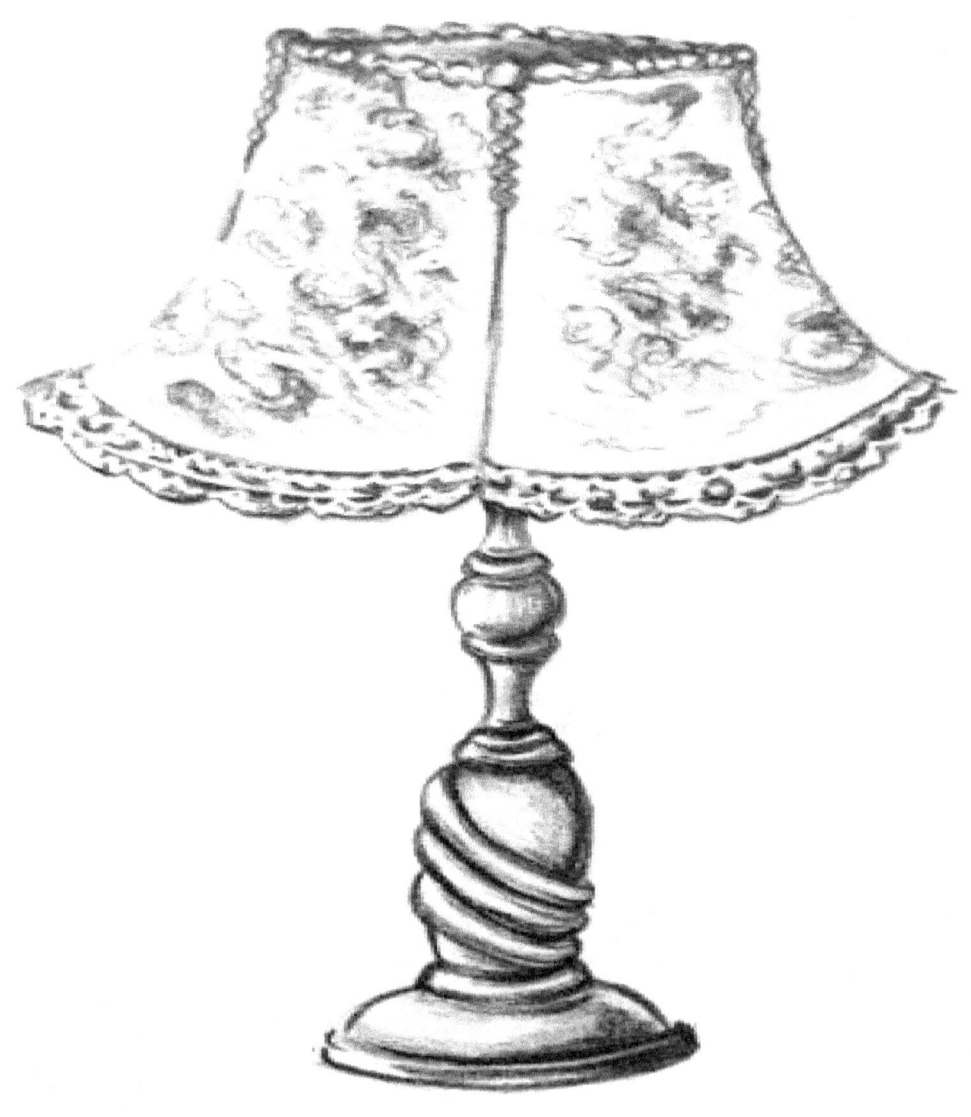

Chapter 2 How to draw Dream Catcher

Step 1

We are going to draw a wheel of a Dream Catcher along with a few embellishments including some feathers. Everybody knows how Dream Catchers look like and here we will learn how to draw one of them.

Draw a wheel in the center of the page. Draw three circles overlapping each other's boundaries. Note that the outlines are drawn roughly thick.

Fill up the core of the overlapping circles with shading. Leave a white spot blank.

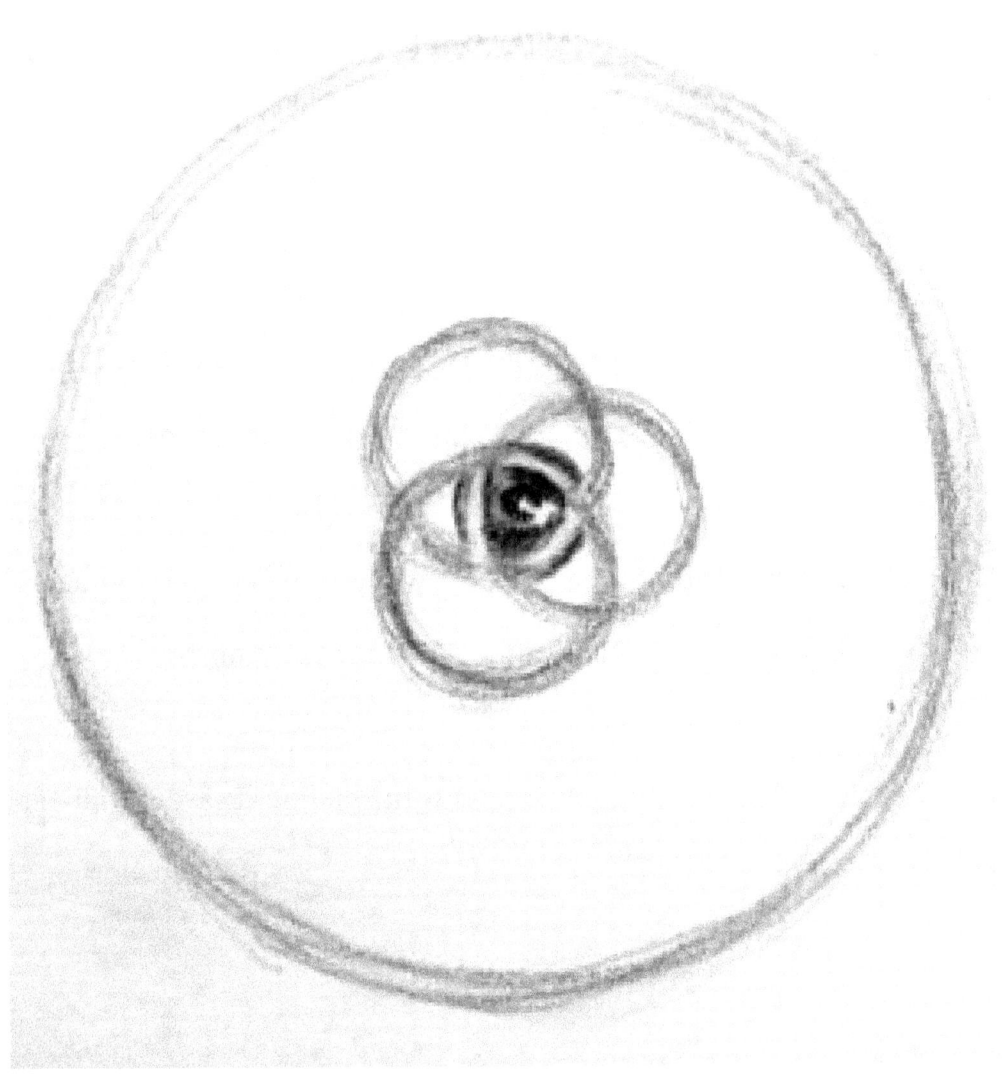

Step 2

Draw the final dark outline in the form of concentric circles for all the circles, the largest circle as well as the overlapping circles.

Draw a ribbon swirling around the bigger circle.

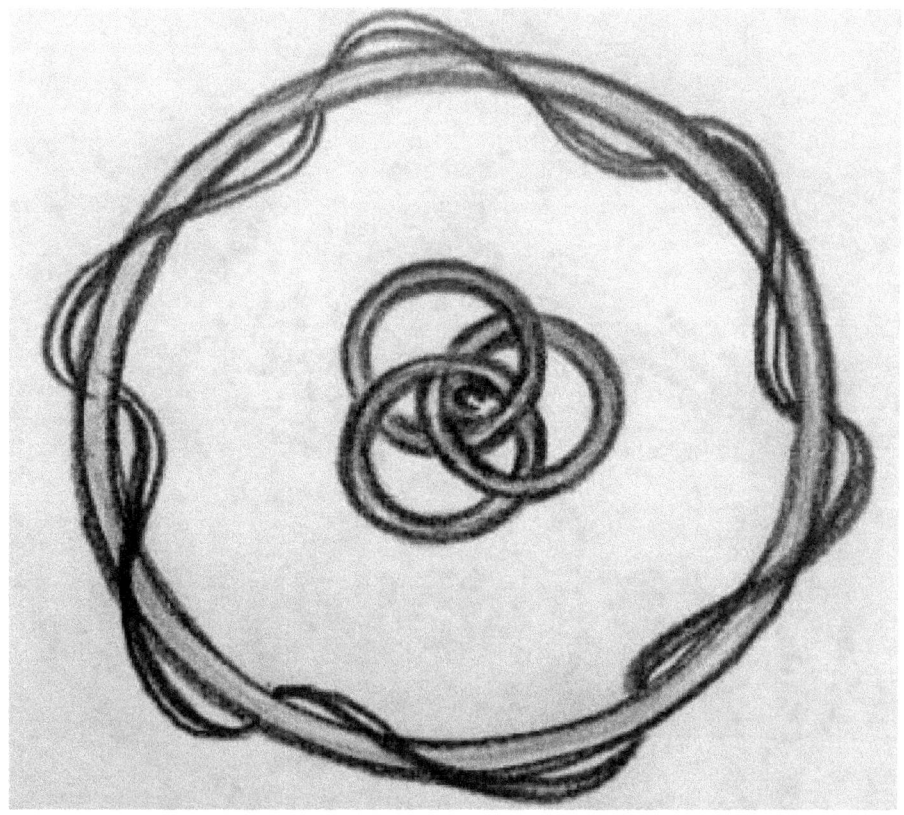

Step 3

Using white poster color or white pencil, highlight some joints on the wheel. This gives the suggestion of the presence of some metal fixtures on the wheel. Do the same for the joints of overlapping circles.

Draw some more ribbons coming out of the inner circles and joining to the wheel.

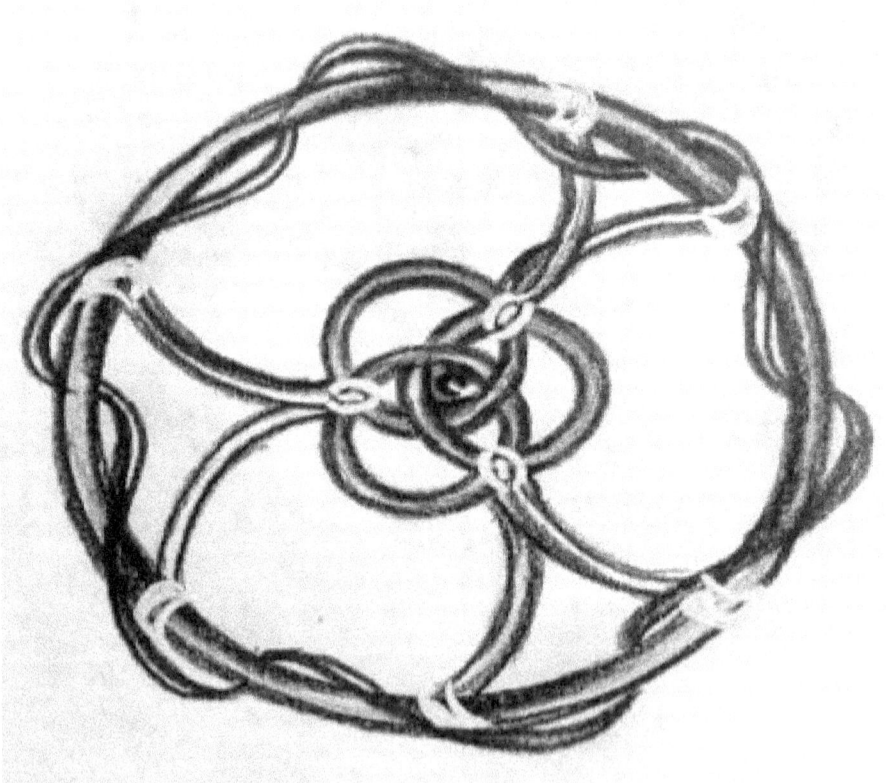

Step 4

Draw some curved lines from the wheel moving towards the center in such a manner that they give the idea of claws.

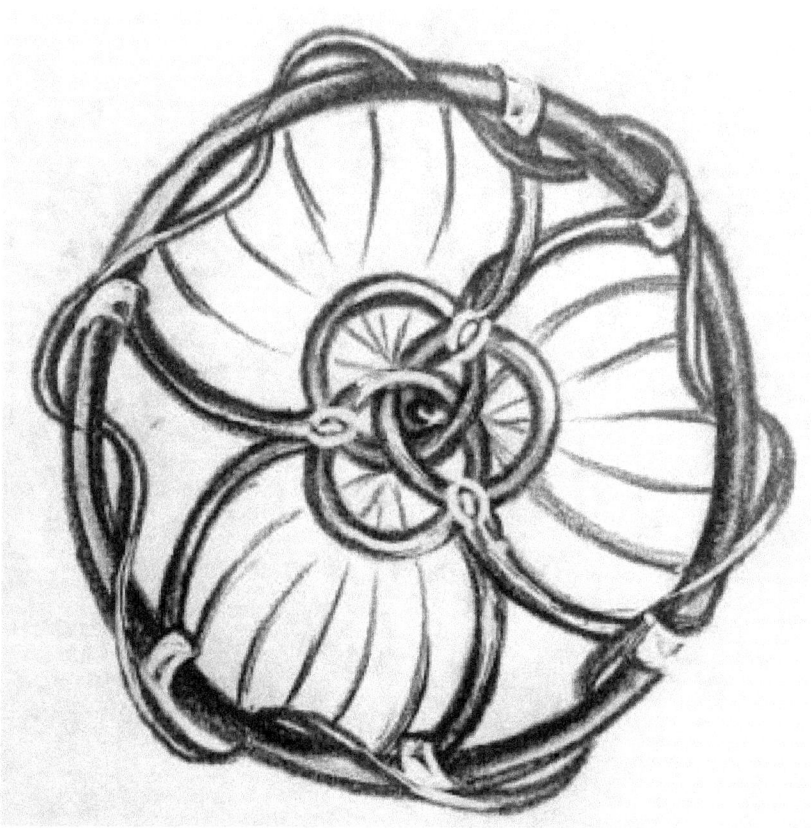

Step 5

From one of the lowermost metal fixtures, draw a bell hanging downwards.
The bell is joined to the metal with a loop.

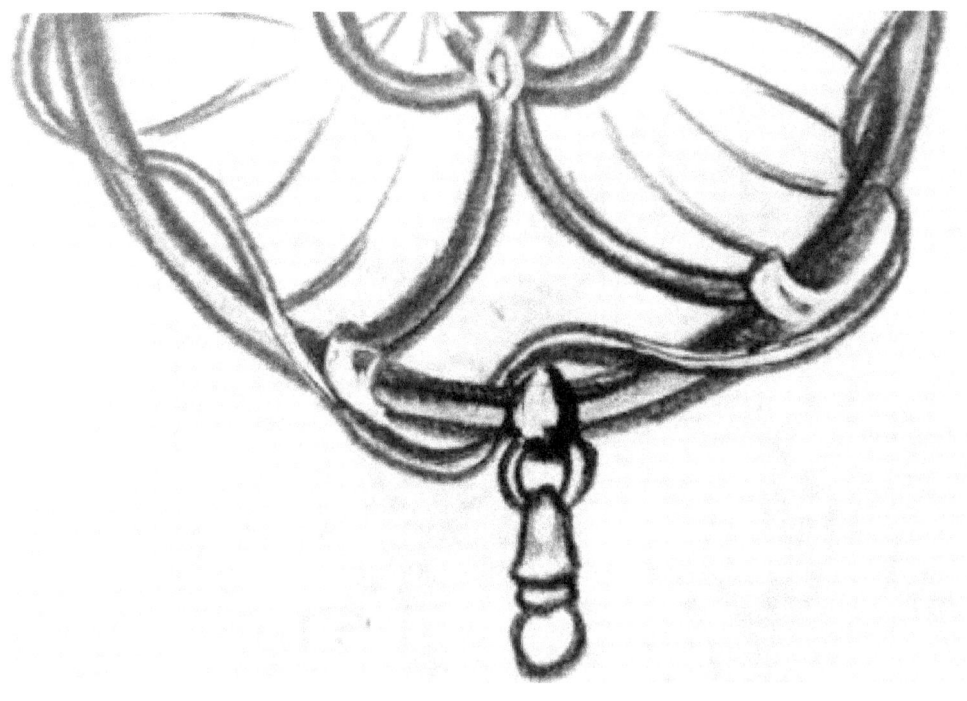

Step 6

Like we did in the previous step; draw two more hanging embellishments from the metal fixtures.

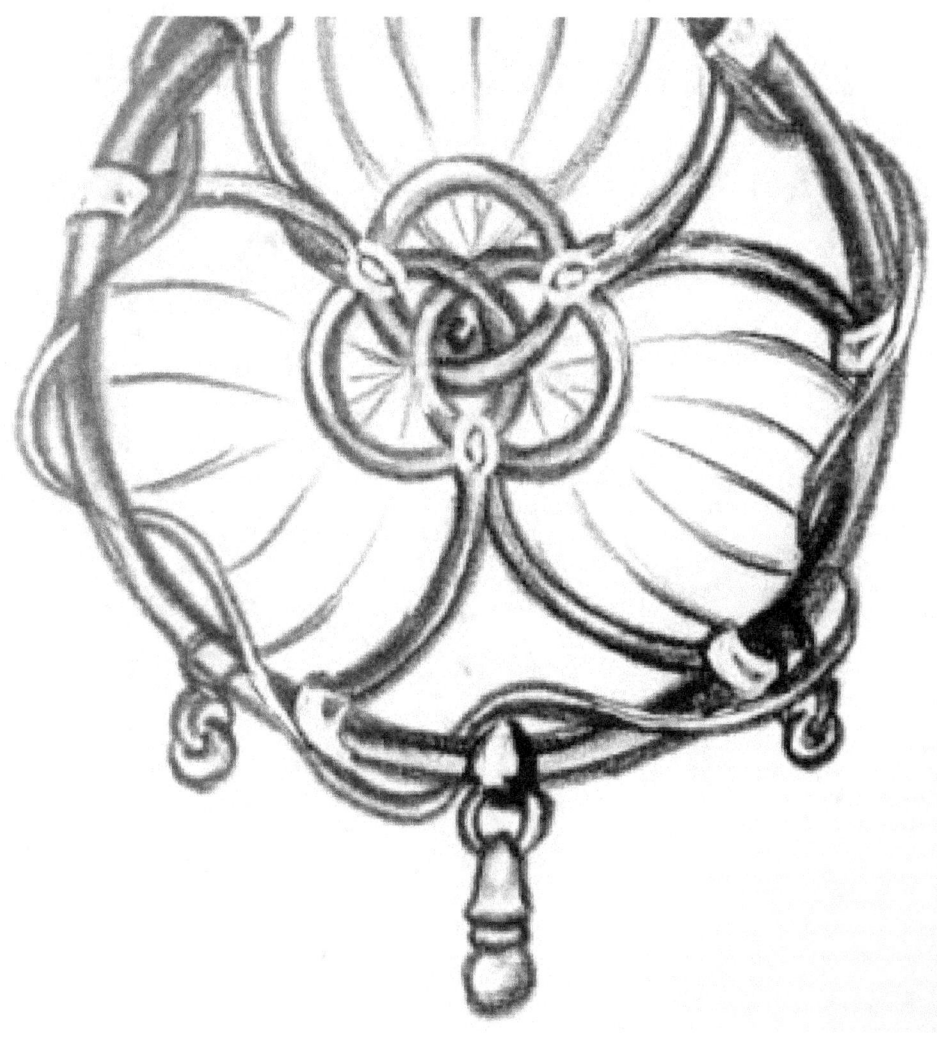

Step 7

Draw the shaft of feathers with scribbled lines from all the three hangings.

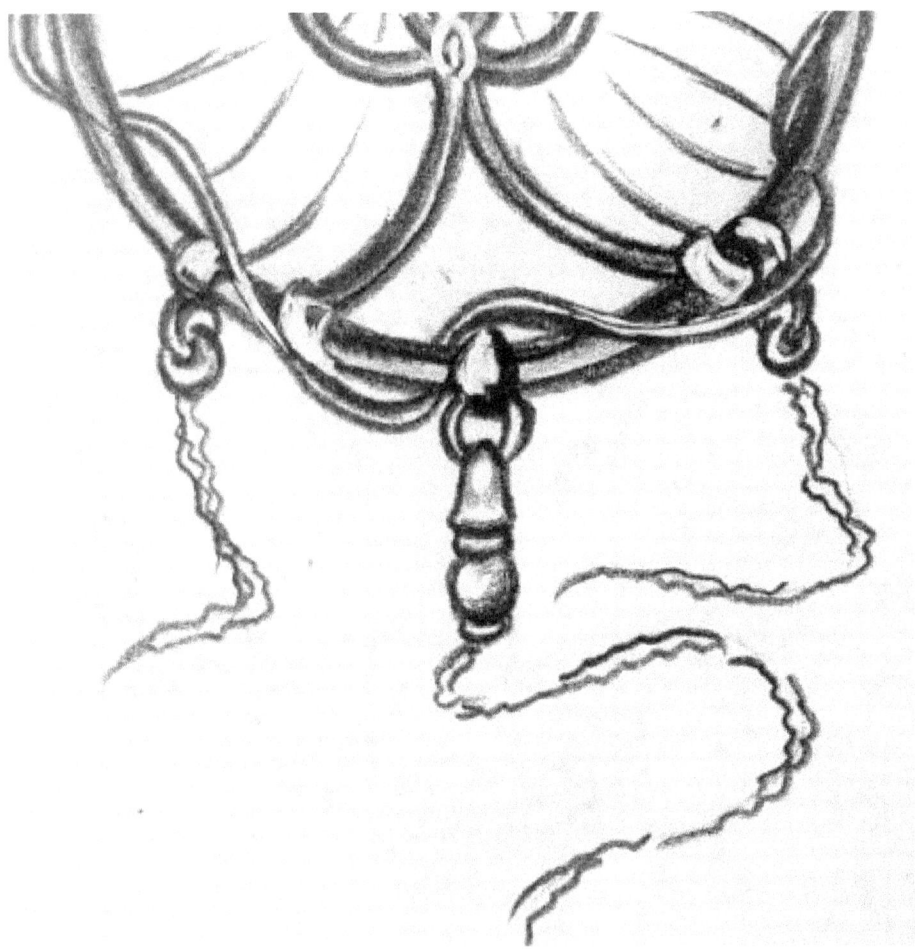

Step 8

Draw a few lines for outer barbs and down barb of the feather in the center.

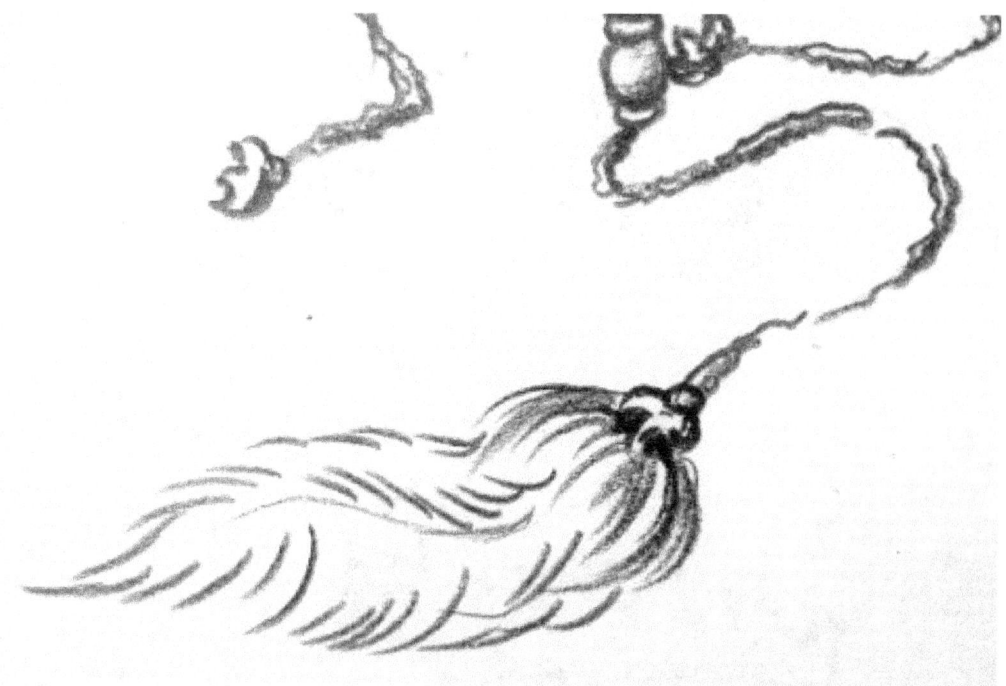

Step 9

Complete the feather with barb. Give shading with the lines of a blunt pencil only.

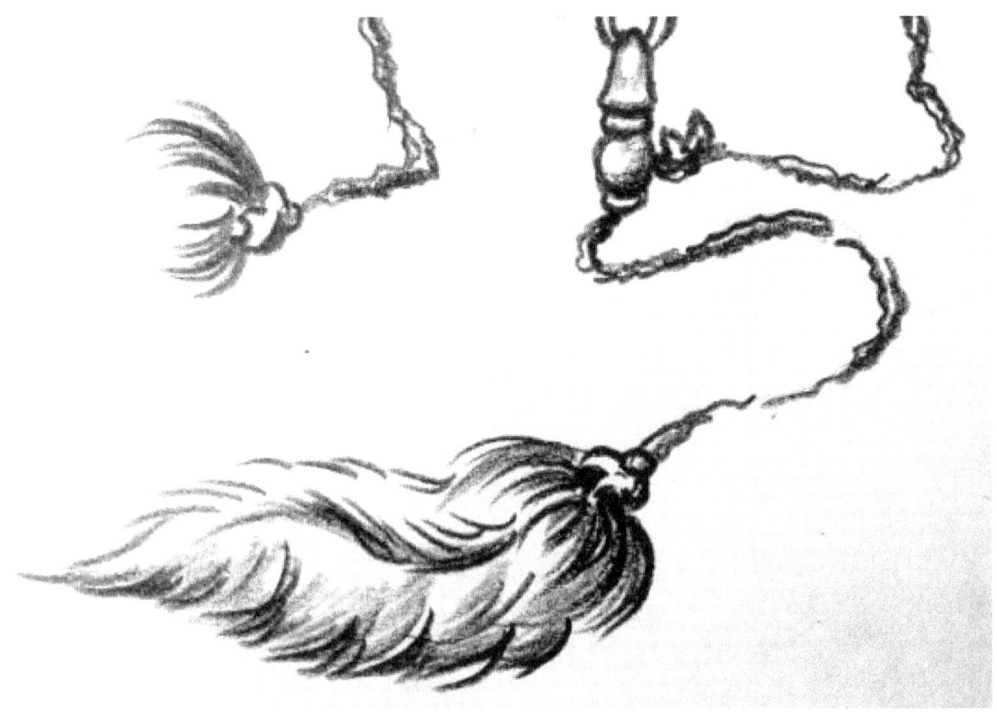

Step 10

Just we drew the middle feather, draw the other two feathers as well, hanging from the loops.

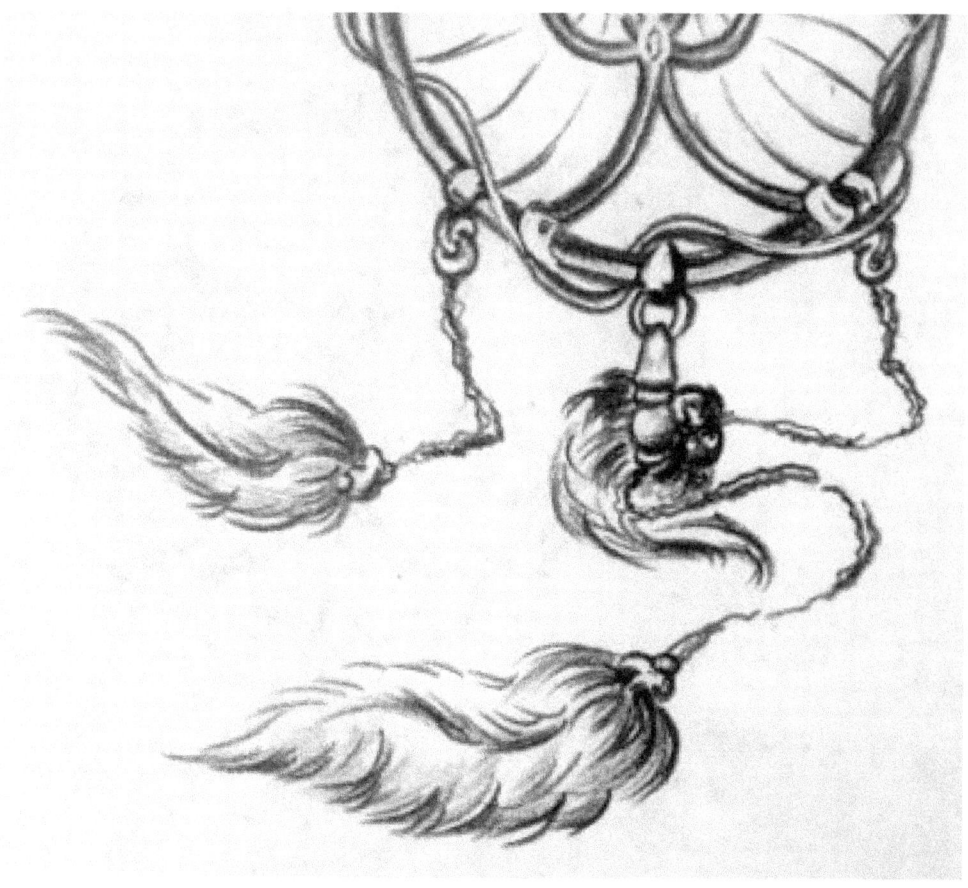

Step 11

Give finishing touches to the wheel and feathers. Complete the drawing of the Dream Catcher.

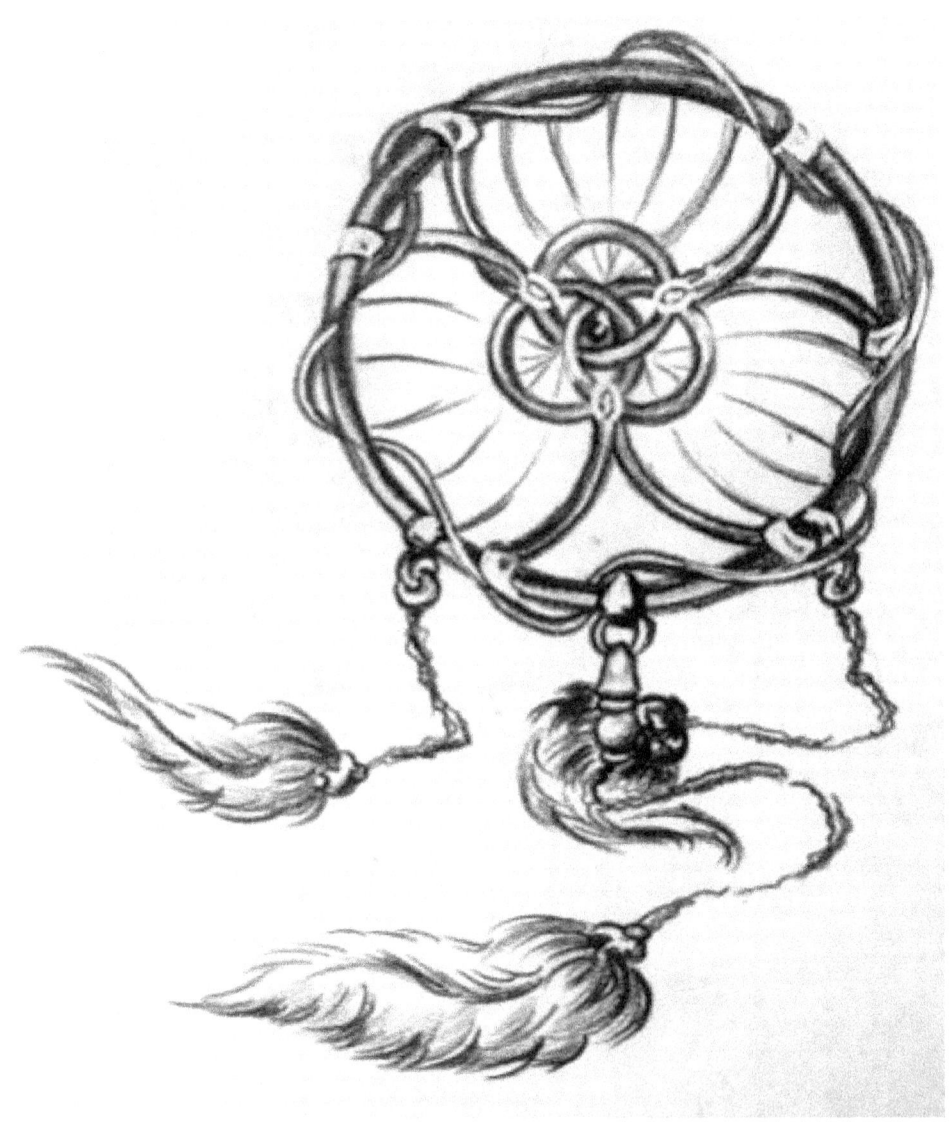

Chapter 3 How to draw a Violoncello

Step 1

We are going to draw an embellished Violoncello. It would look superb in the hands of any musician. Draw the light outlines of the violoncello bent on a violin stand.

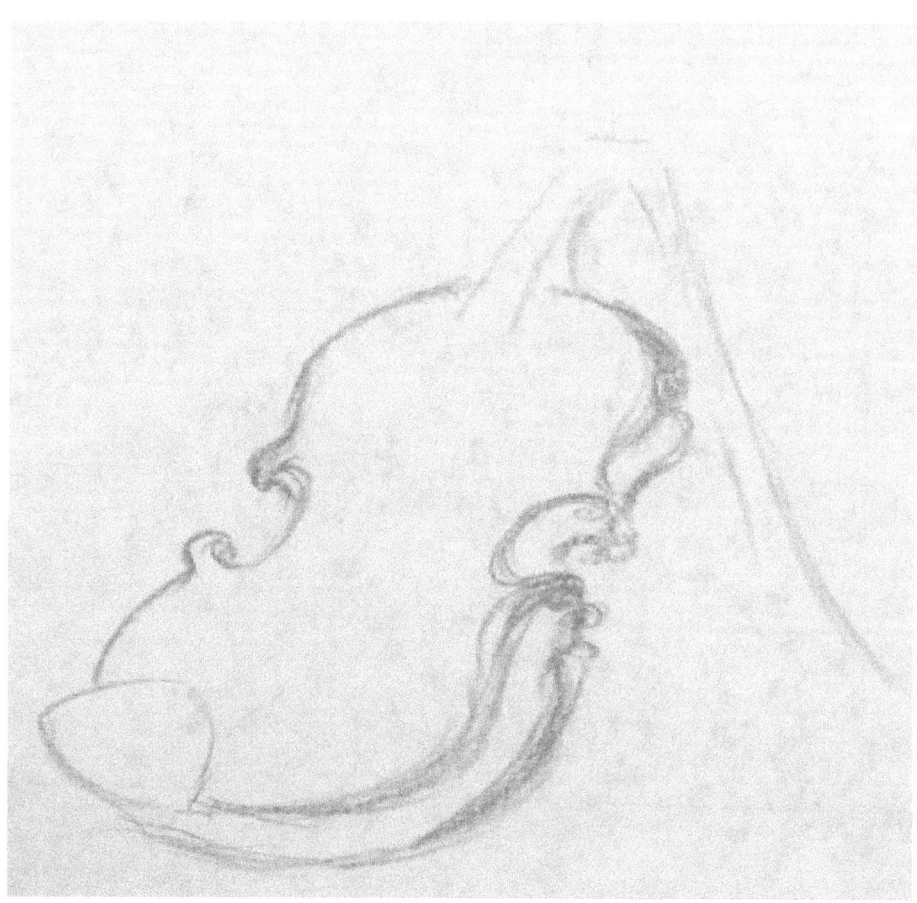

Step 2

Draw a guitar pick in one corner of the violoncello. The pick is drawn somewhat larger in size. The curly design in the body of the violoncello is also given a little highlight in this step. Since it is a designer violin, the embellishments are given more emphasis than a regular violoncello.

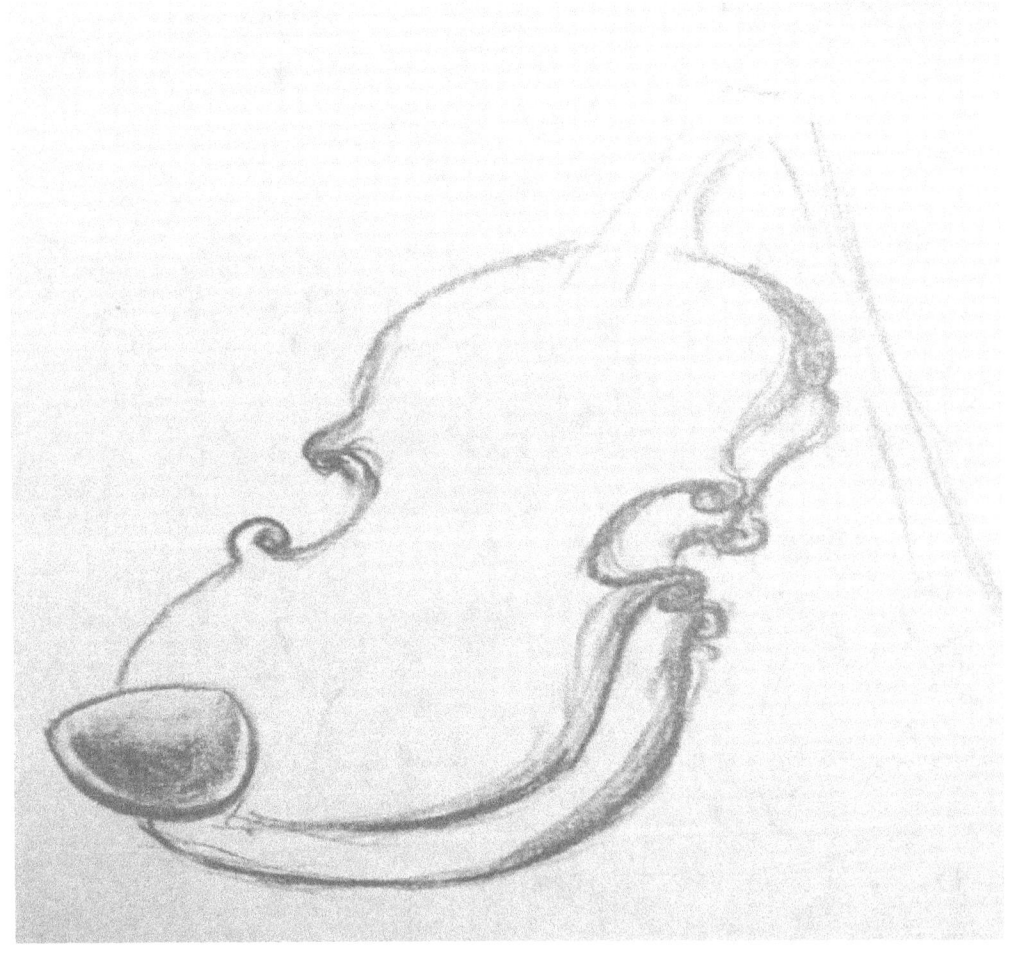

Step 3

Give shading in the rib of the violin. Keep in mind the source of light and the variation in shading. Also draw the end pin and shade it well. Draw the sound board and give some curly lines there.

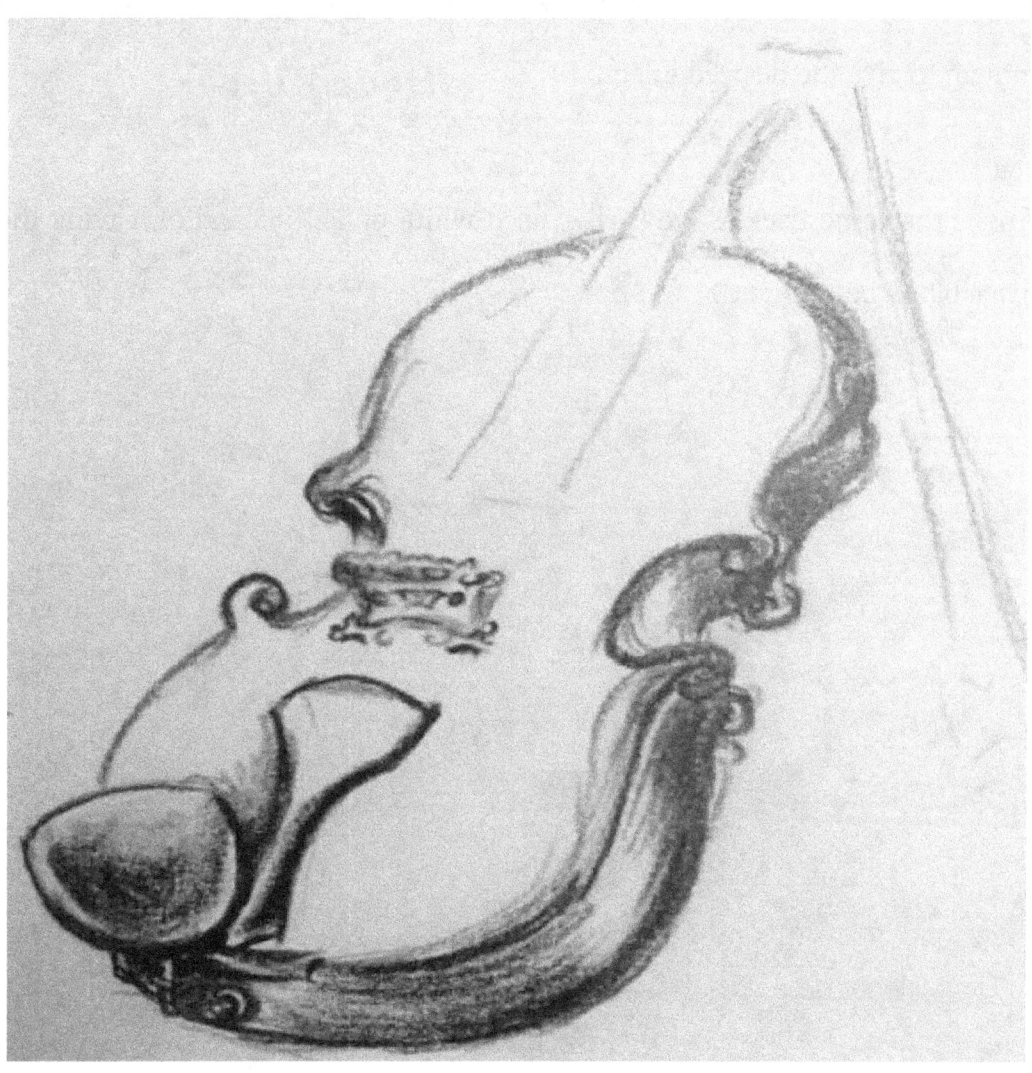

Step 4

Draw some stings passing over the sound board. Draw some designs on the body of the violoncello for decorating it. You can also use a black sketch pen for creating a dramatic effect with pencil. The black sketch pen or marker is used sometimes in pencil shading when the extreme dark pencils are not enough to give the desired effect.

This is the same trick as we earlier used white pencil instead of leaving the space blank beforehand.

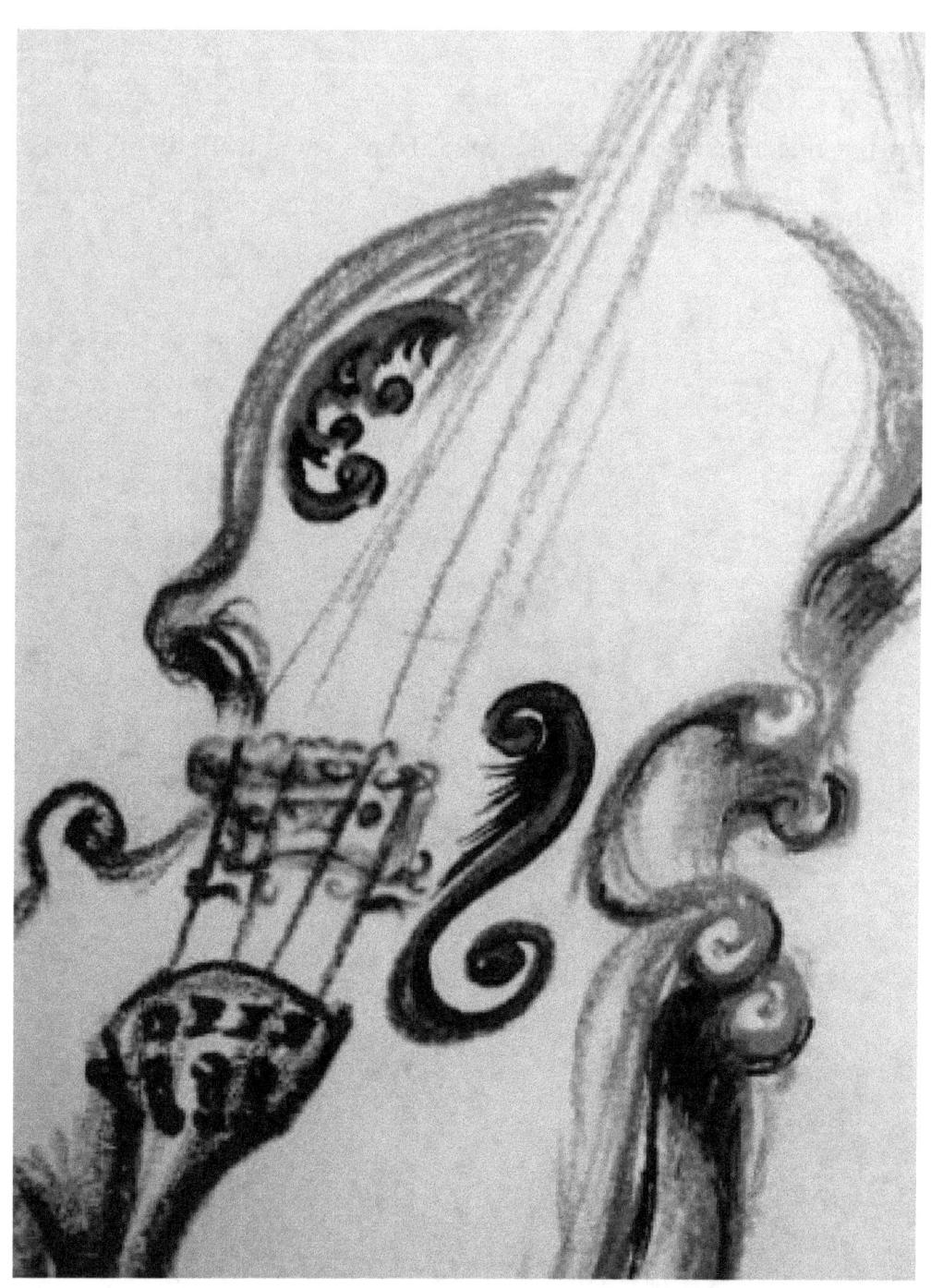

Step 5

Draw the fingerboard of the violoncello. Leave some white blank space to create the effect of reflection of light.

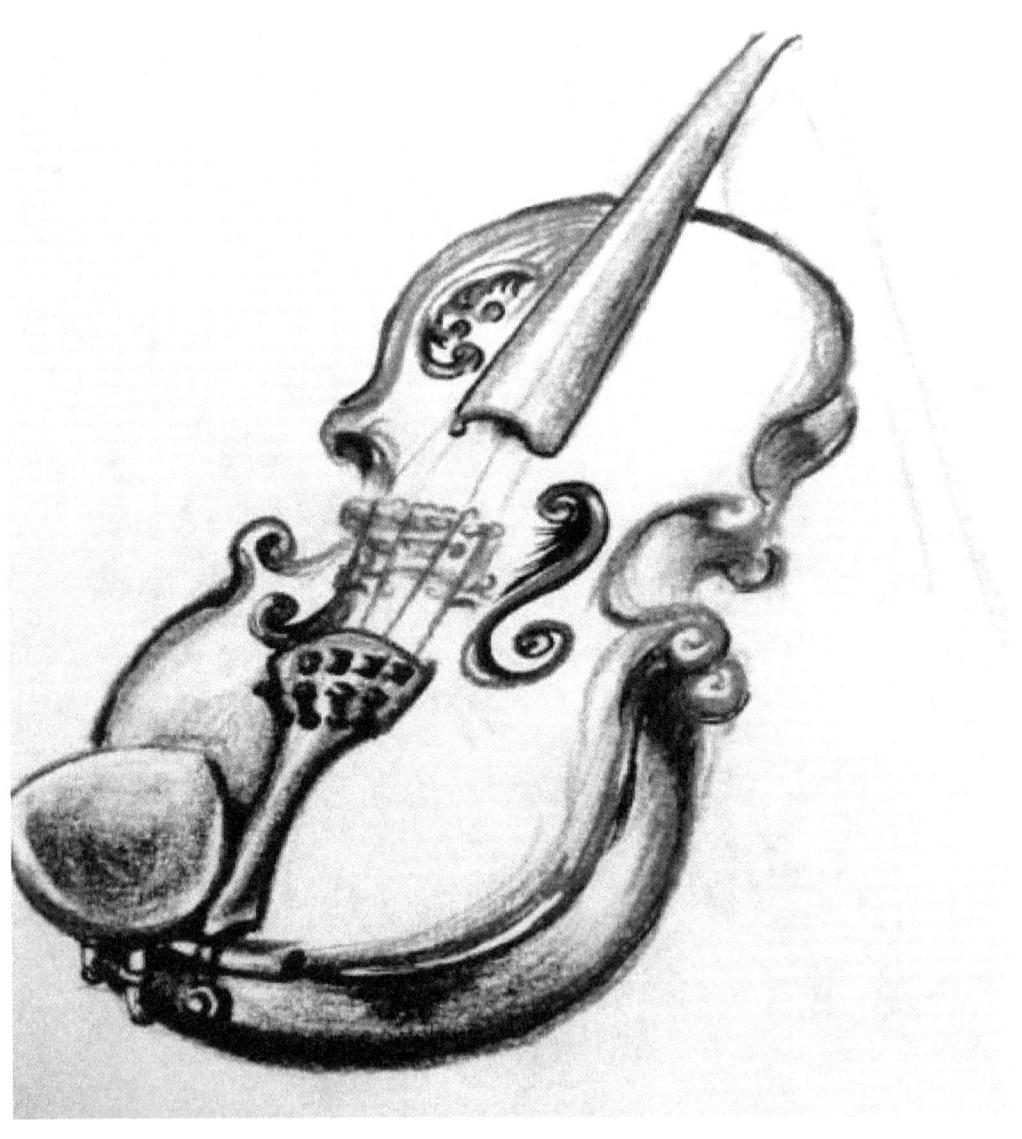

Step 6

To shade the body of the violoncello, two steps are needed. Firstly, shade the upper bout and lower bout with a blunt pencil. Now using a very sharp and dark pencil, create some vertical lines over the shading. These sharp lines give the finished effect to the drawing. This technique is also called hatching.

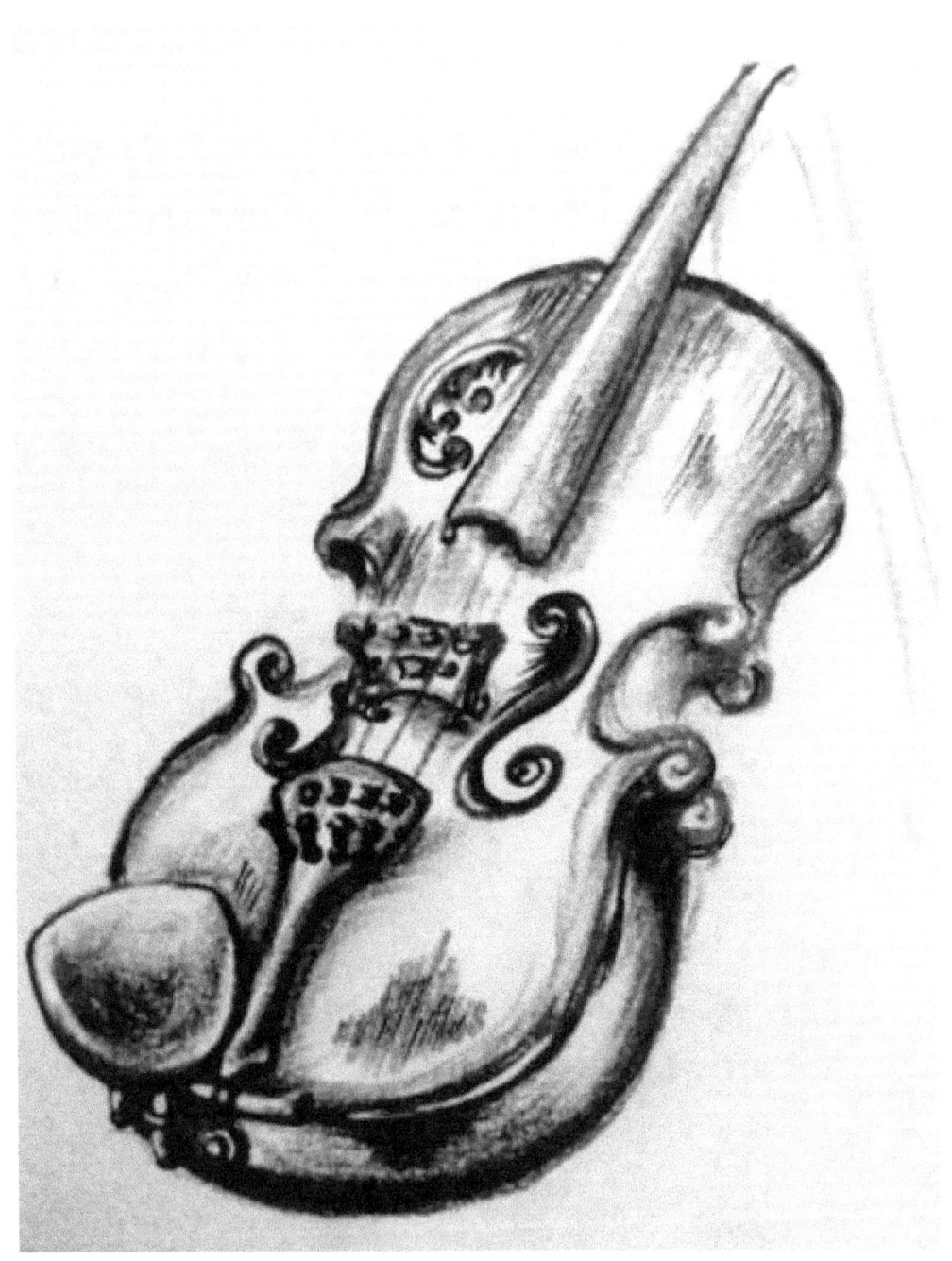

Step 7

Give finishing to the head of the violoncello. Draw a cello stand, with the help of which this violoncello is shown standing. Notice the difference in gradations of shading within a single cello stand only.

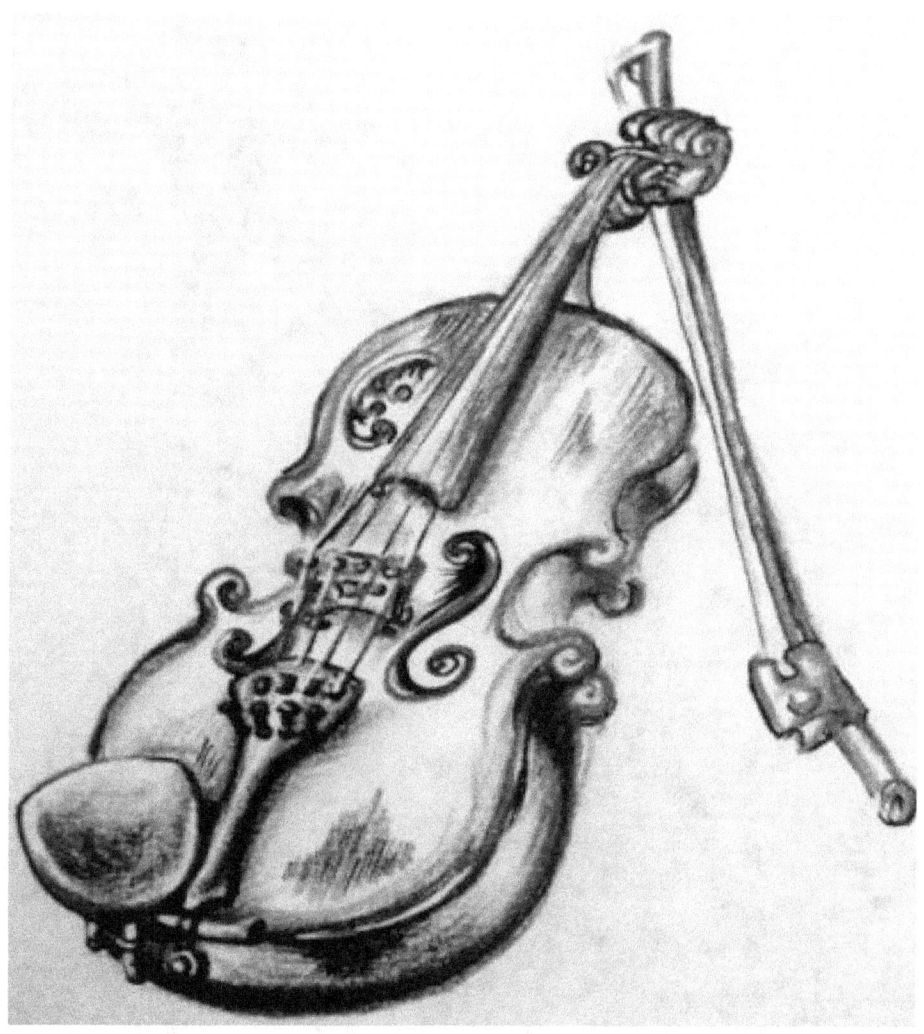

Step 8

Give shading to the ground on which the violoncello is standing. Give finishing touches to the violoncello and complete the drawing.

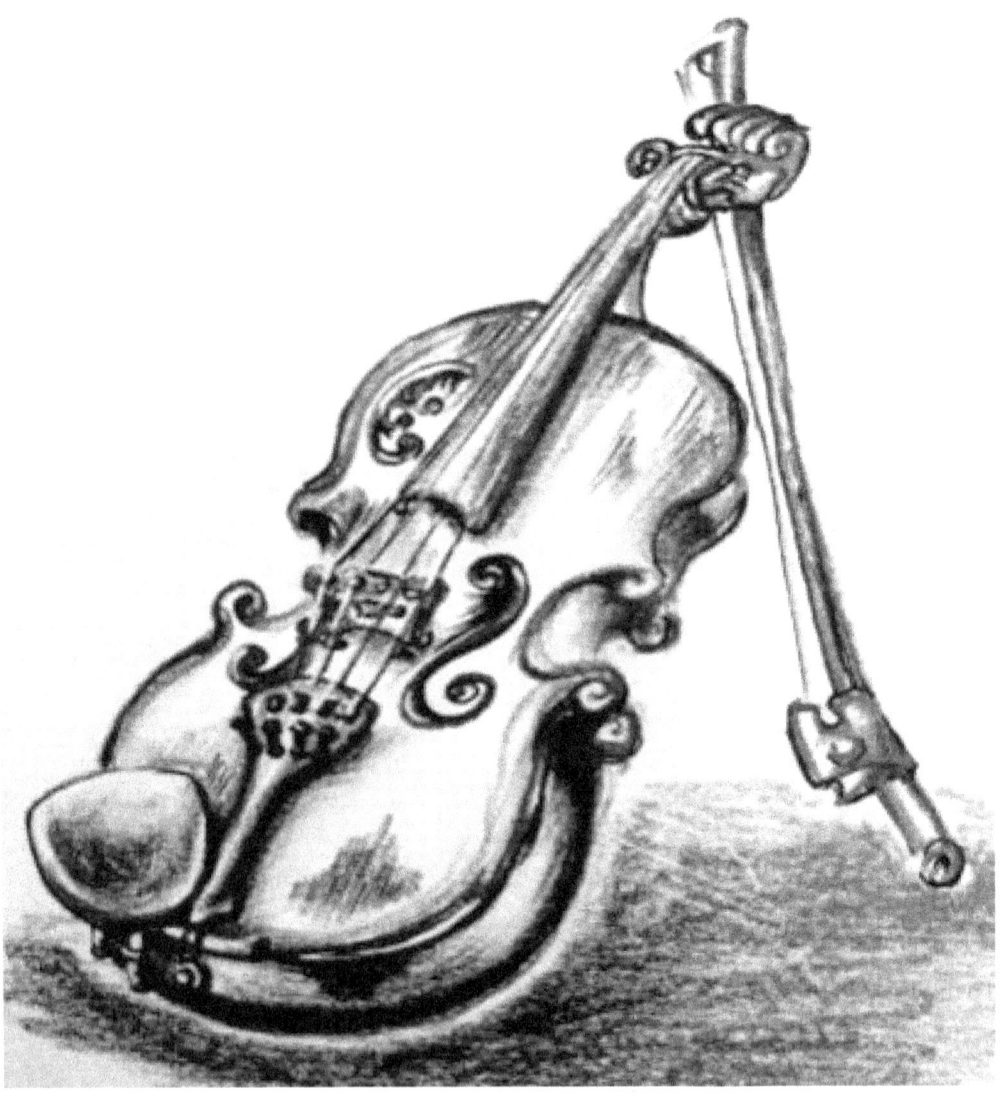

Chapter 4 How to draw a Baby Donkey

Step 1

The next drawing in the series of cool drawings is the sletch of a baby donkey. We have to draw the whole body of the toy but we will start with the face.

Draw the face of the donkey. The mouth of the animal is shown protruding outwards.

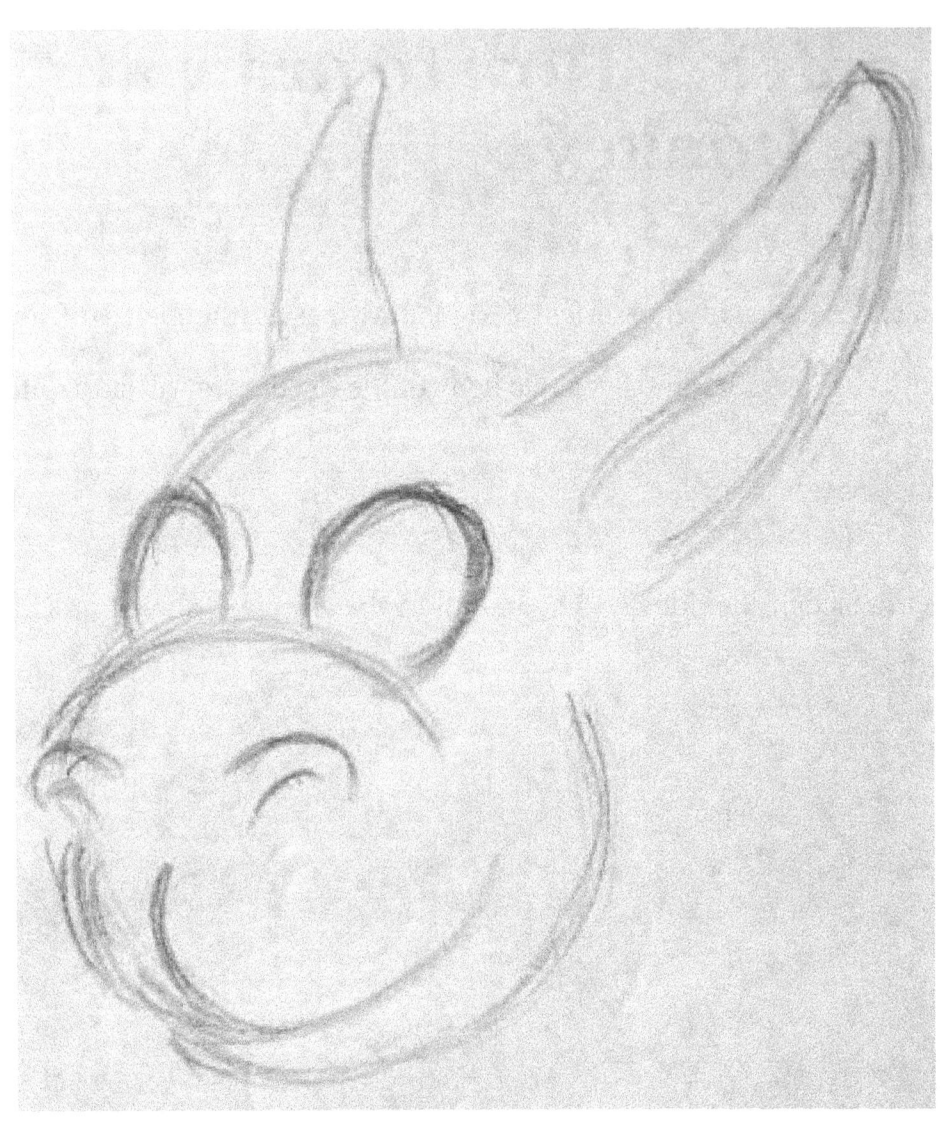

Step 2

Draw some hair on the head of the donkey. Since it is a toy, we will show some stitches wherever required. Draw a few stitches on one of the horns, in the middle of the eyes and over the upper lip. The donkey is smiling at someone.

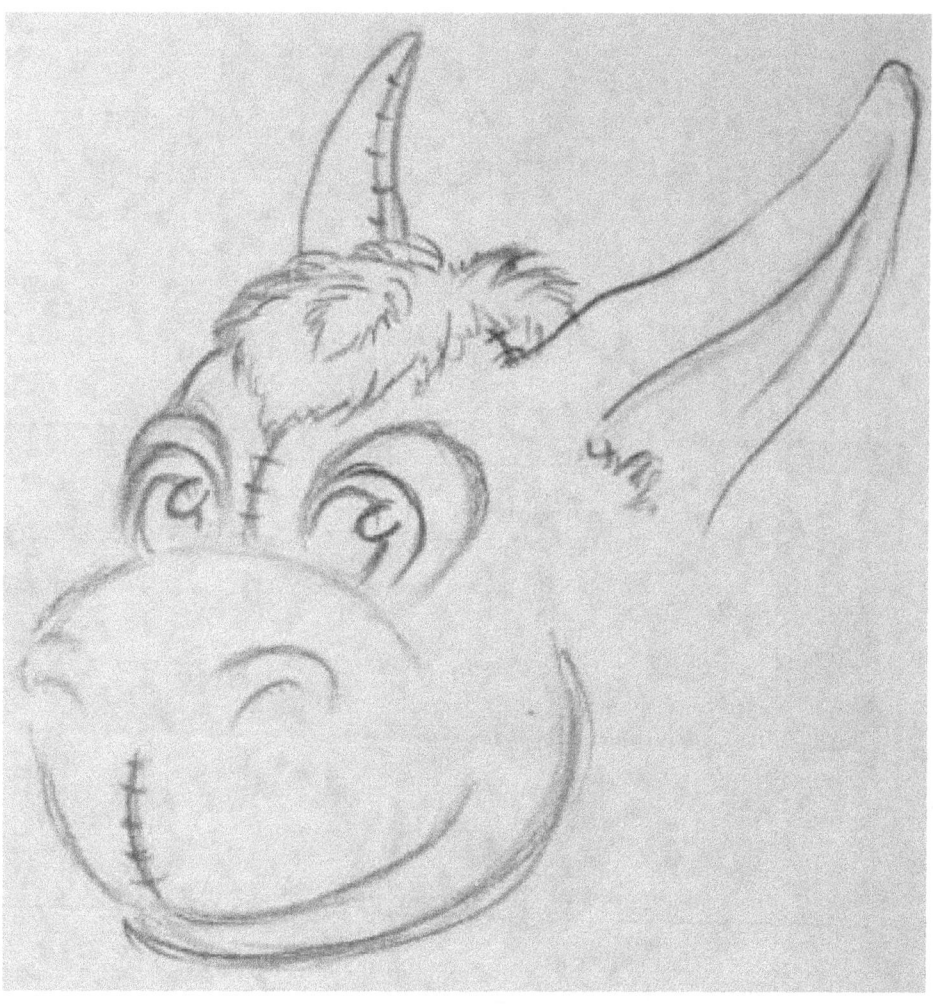

Step 3

Give shading in the large eyes of the donkey. Leave two white spaces in the eyes in the white portion. This white space is left blank to denote glitter in the eyes. Moreover, it is a baby animal, we have exaggerated the size of the head, eyes and of the glitter as well.

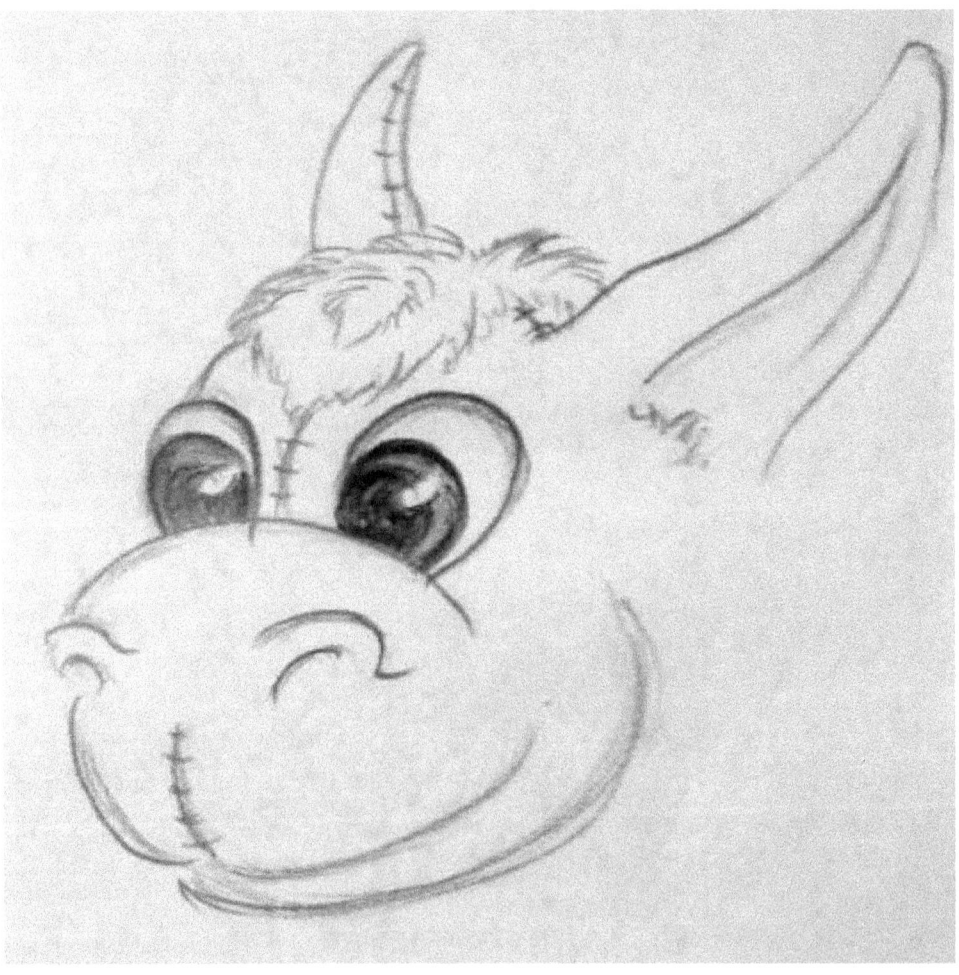

Step 4

Draw the rest of the body of the sitting donkey. The tail of the animal is drawn like a pom-pom.

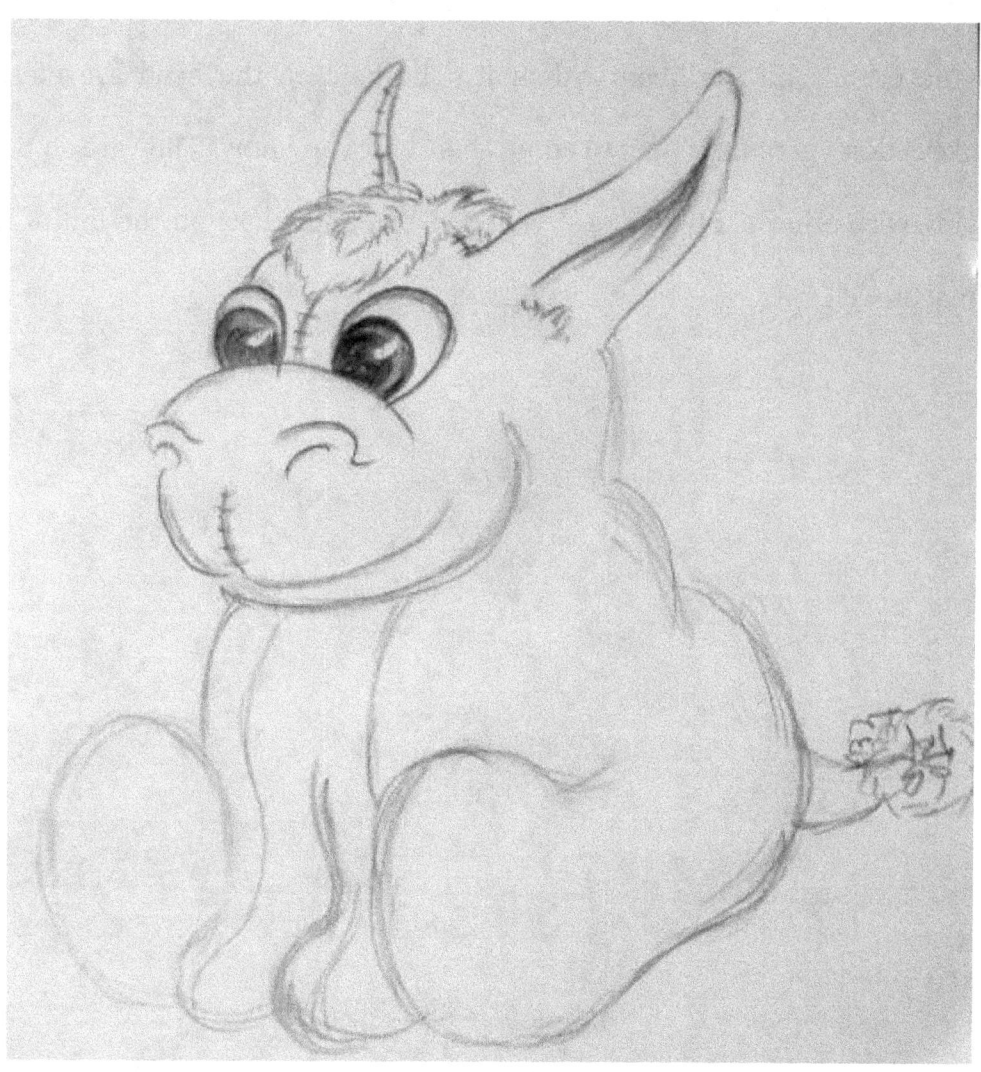

Step 5

Give some light shading in the horns of the baby donkey and in its mouth also.

Fill the outline on the head with hair. The hair on the head are messy. Donkeys don't get much time to comb their hair you know! They are so busy playing with other baby donkeys! Wink! Draw some hair on the tail of the animal as well.

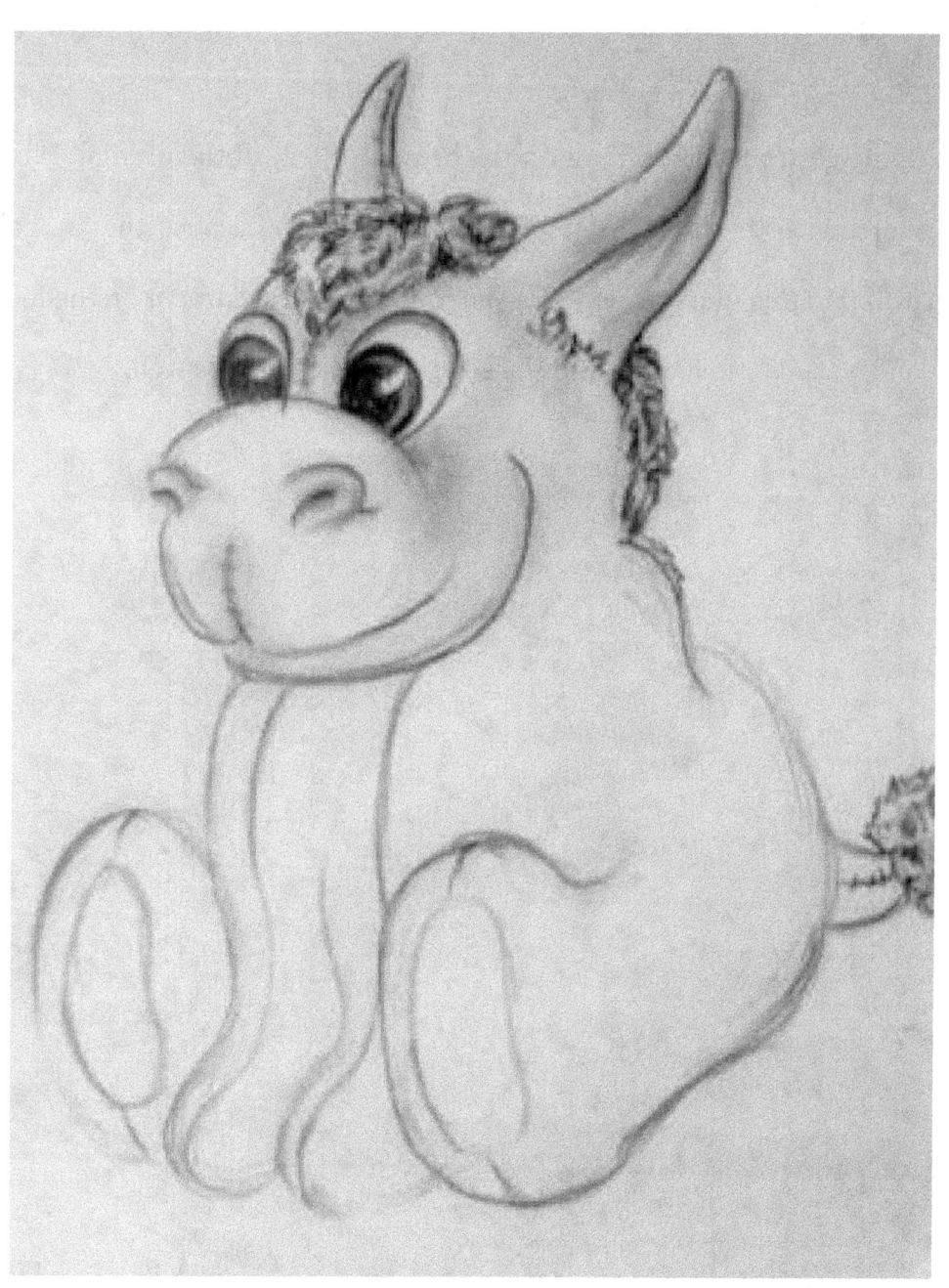

Step 6

Give some gestures of stitching on the arms and feet of the animal. We are not referring to the limbs as forelegs and hind legs because the animal is humanized in this illustration. Give shading in the ovals drawn on the feet of the donkey. Give stitches around the edges of these ovals as well.

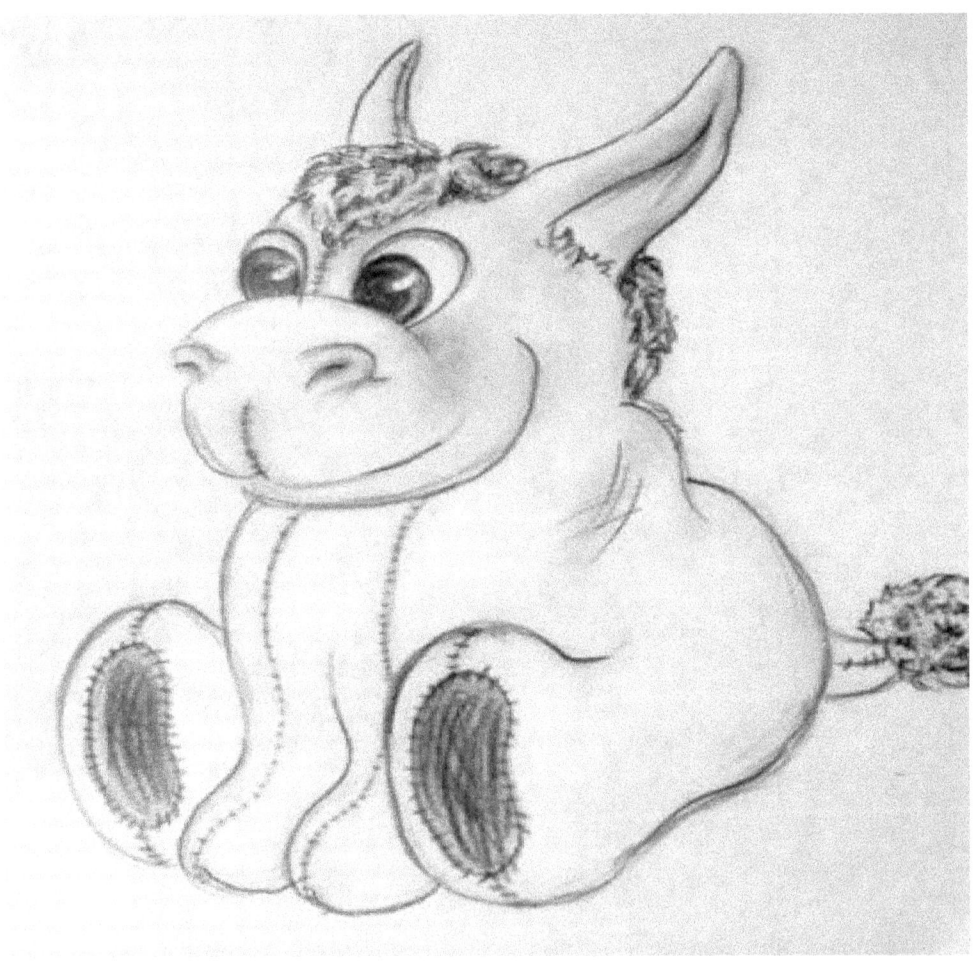

Step 7

Give shading in the nostrils of the donkey. Smudge the graphite well throughout the body of the donkey but the shading should be very light. Give finishing touches to the illustration to complete the baby donkey.

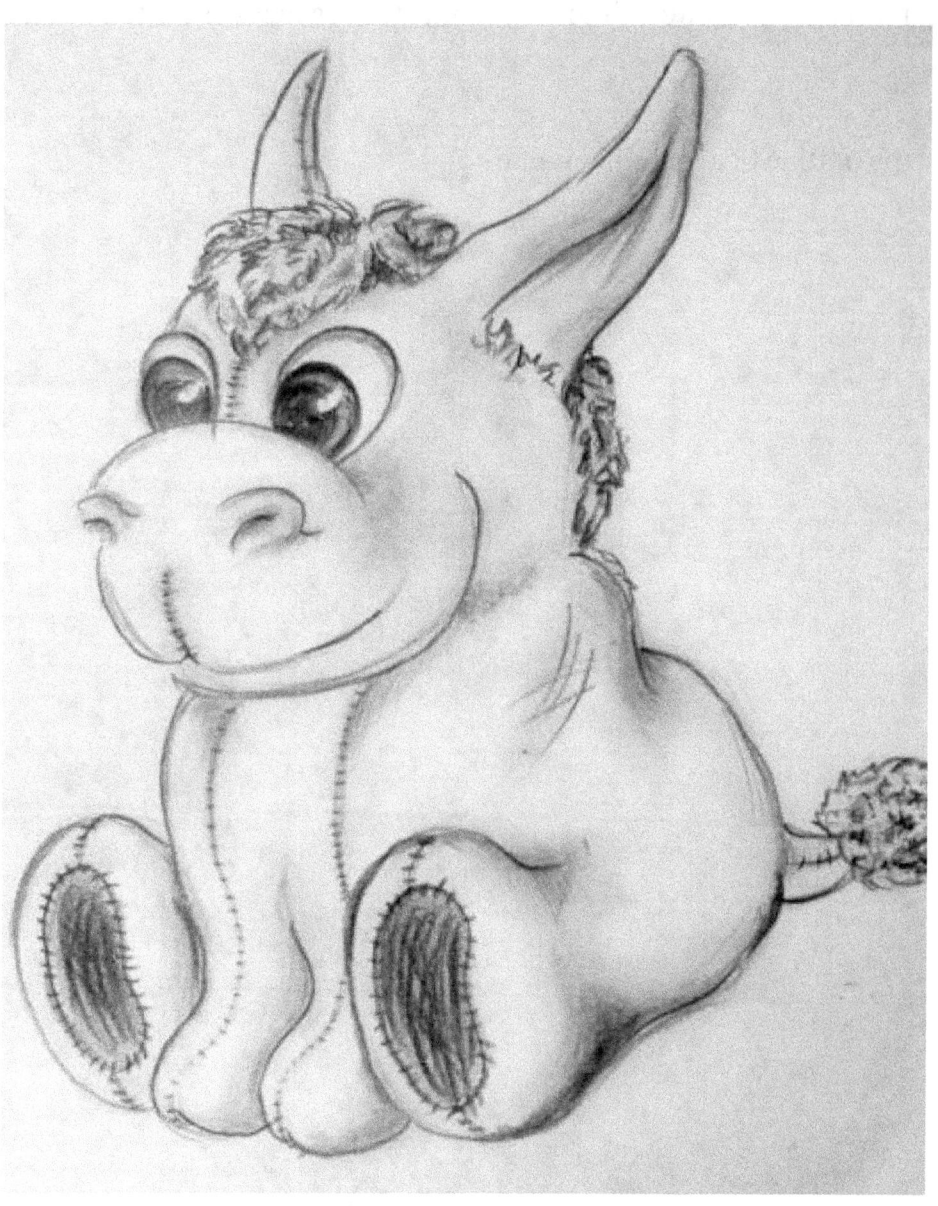

Chapter 5 How to draw a Guitar in the Corner

Step 1

In the earlier chapter, we had drawn a guitar standing along a guitar stand.

Here, in this chapter, we will draw a guitar resting against a wall.

Draw the outline of a standing guitar.

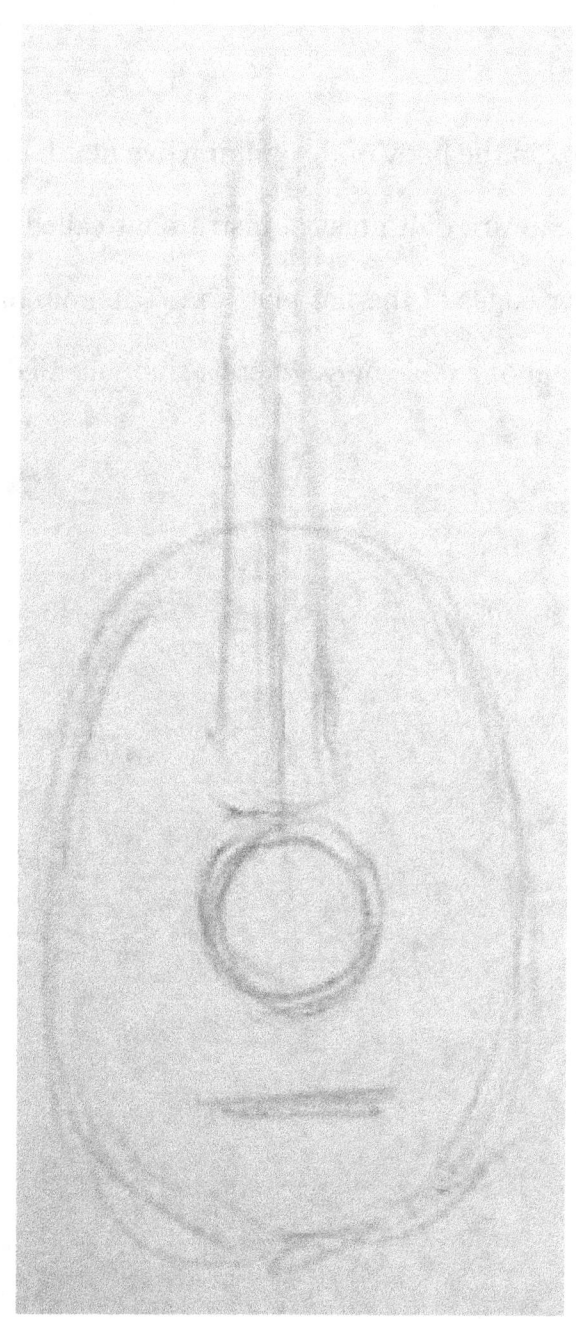

Step 2

Draw the sound box in the body of the guitar. Give depth in the form of dark shading. If you are aware of a musical instrument called "table", you must have seen the outer edges of the flat platform. The boundary of this sound box is drawn like that of a table only, where a ribbon is tied around the thick circular mass.

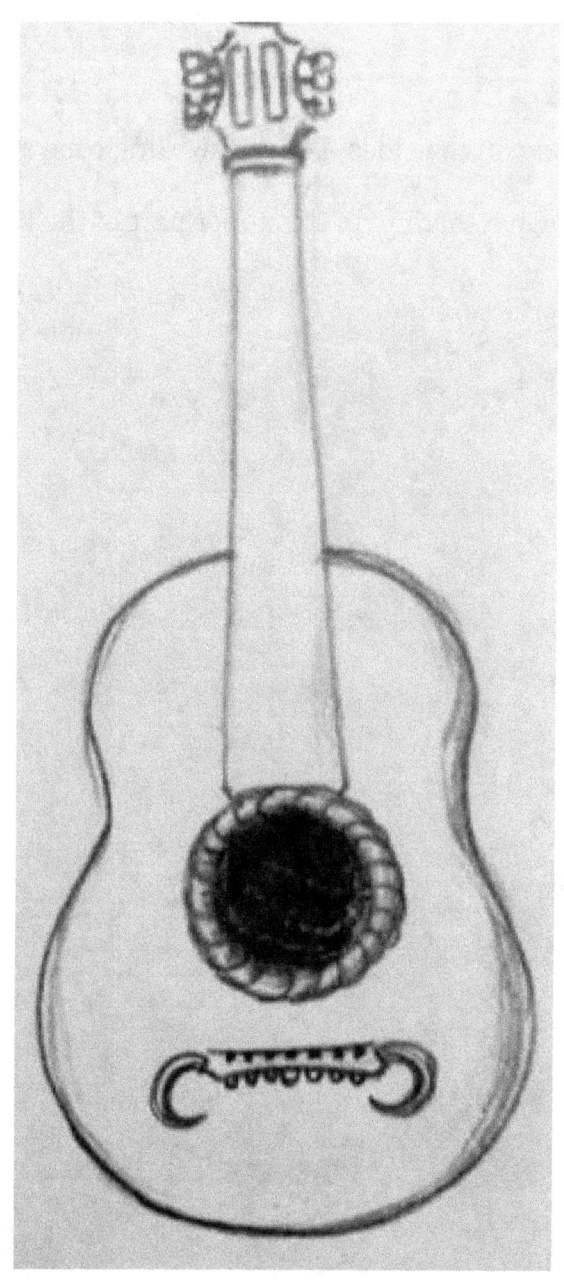

Draw a bridge on the body. The bridge also consists of two horns protruding outwards. Draw the tuning machines on top of the head.

Step 2

Draw ribs of the body on the sides. Draw a swirling rope around the edges of the ribs on the top. Give shading in the upper part of the body.

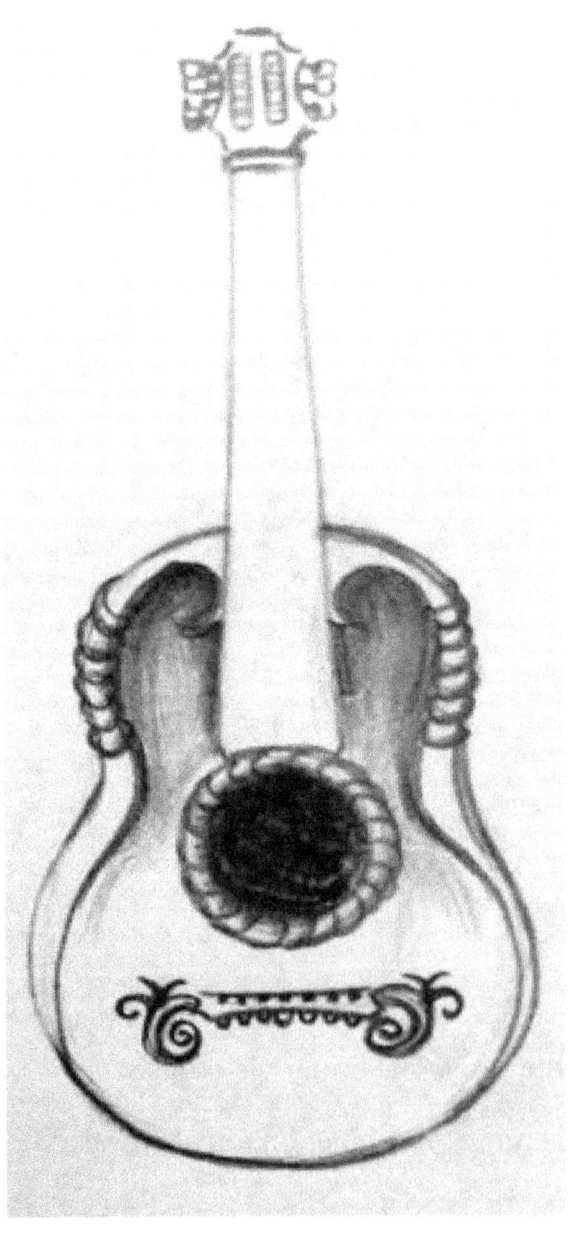

Step 3

Give shading in the lower part of the body. The shading must be done carefully to vary the gradations.

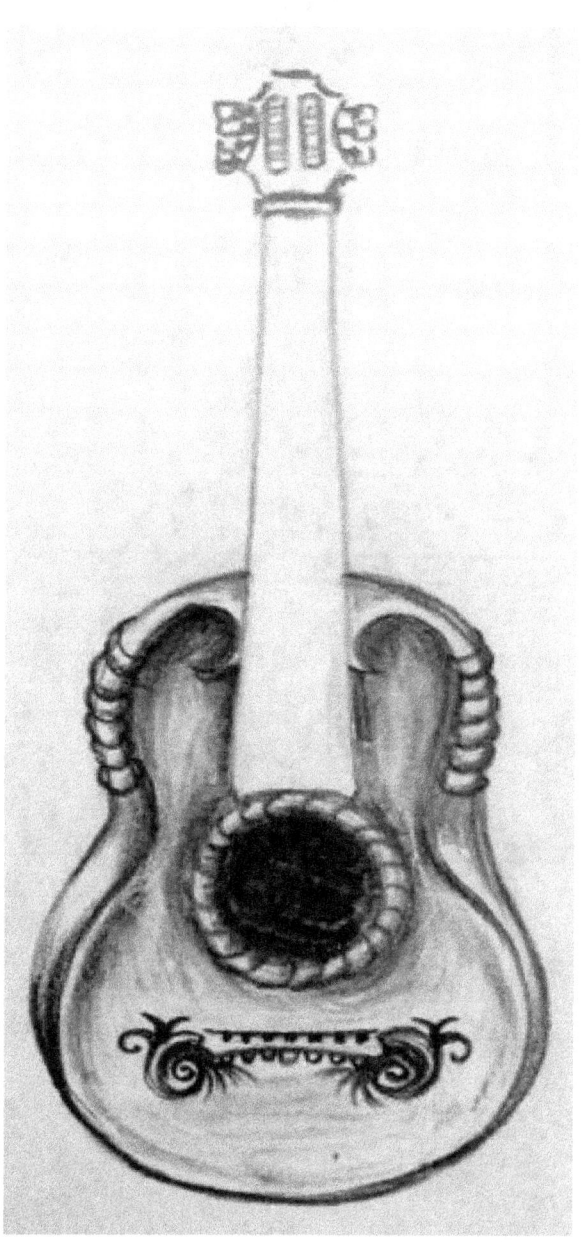

Step 4

Draw the string and soundboard of the guitar. Give shading in this area also.

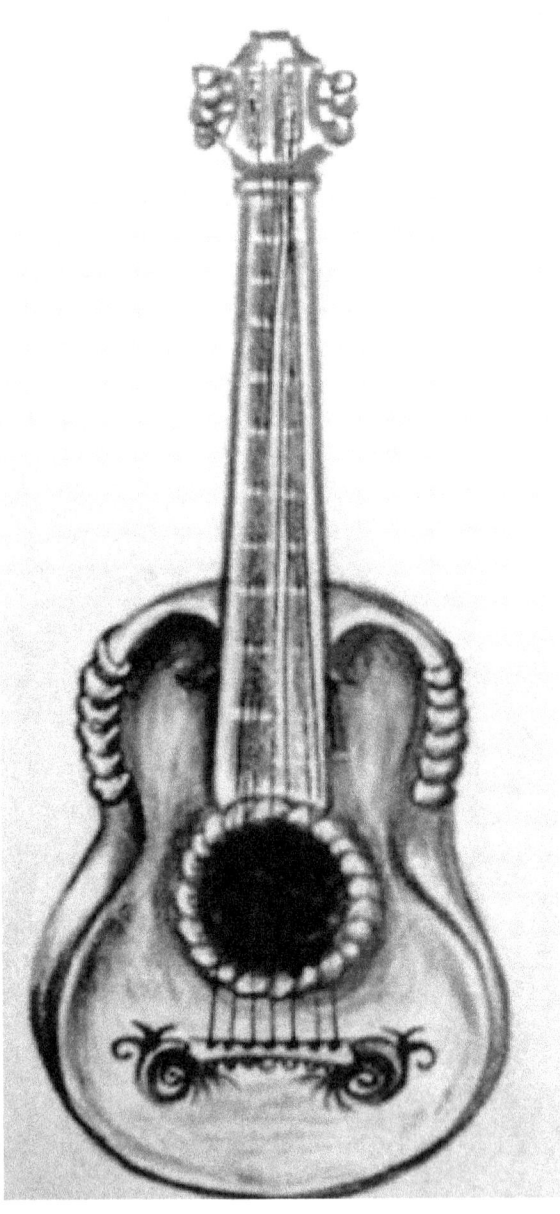

Step 5

Draw two base lines suggesting the presence of a wall behind the guitar. Give shading in the wall around the guitar. Shading the wall gives liveliness to the subject.

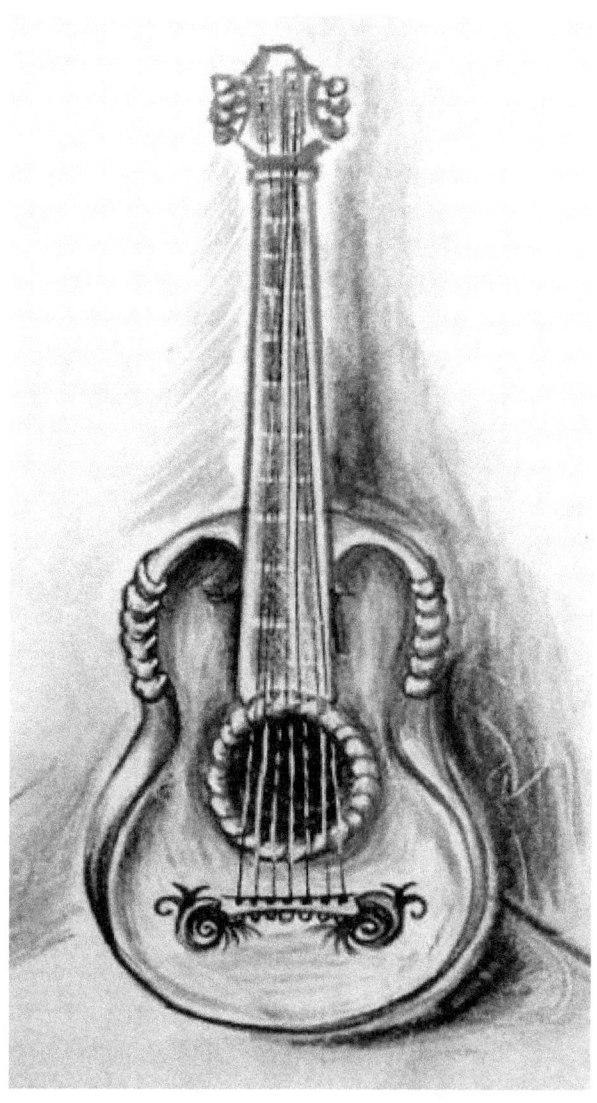

Step 6

The dark and light variations of shading are necessary to make it appealing.

Give finishing touches to the guitar and the wall to complete the illustration.

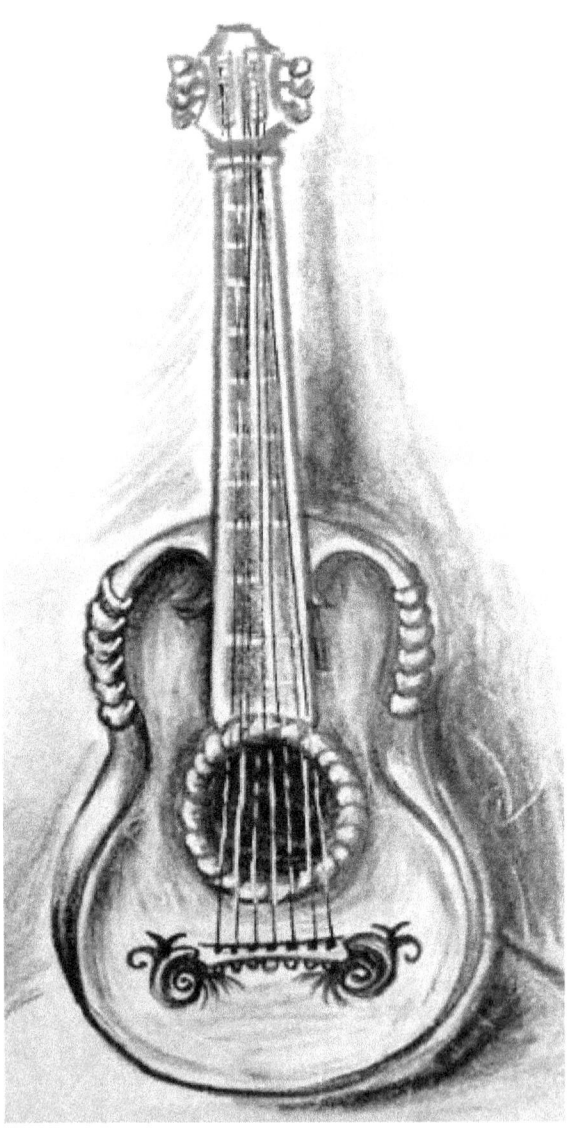

Chapter 6 How to draw a Radio Plane/Drone

Step 1

We are going to draw a kind of imaginary Radio Plane with a central body, four circular rings and rotor blades.

Draw the outline of the Radio Plane- the body, four circular rings and a central oval in each ring. These ovals will be used as guidelines to draw the rotor blades later. Draw the outline with smudged lines. We will carve out the finished outline in the next step.

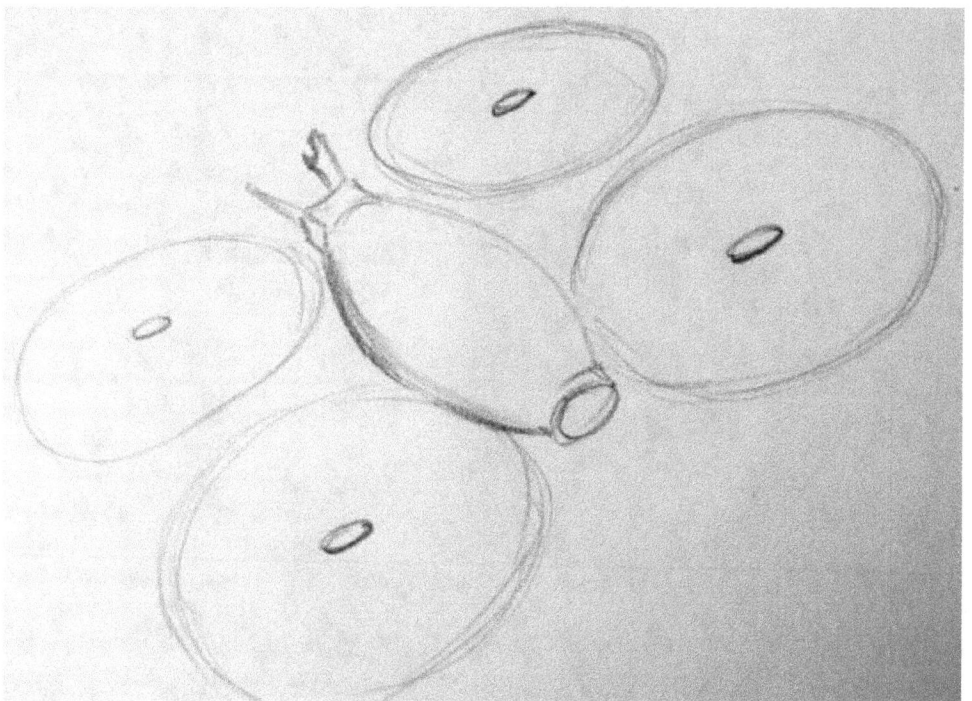

Step 2

Draw the final outline for the body and tail of the drone. The tail is given teeth at its ends.

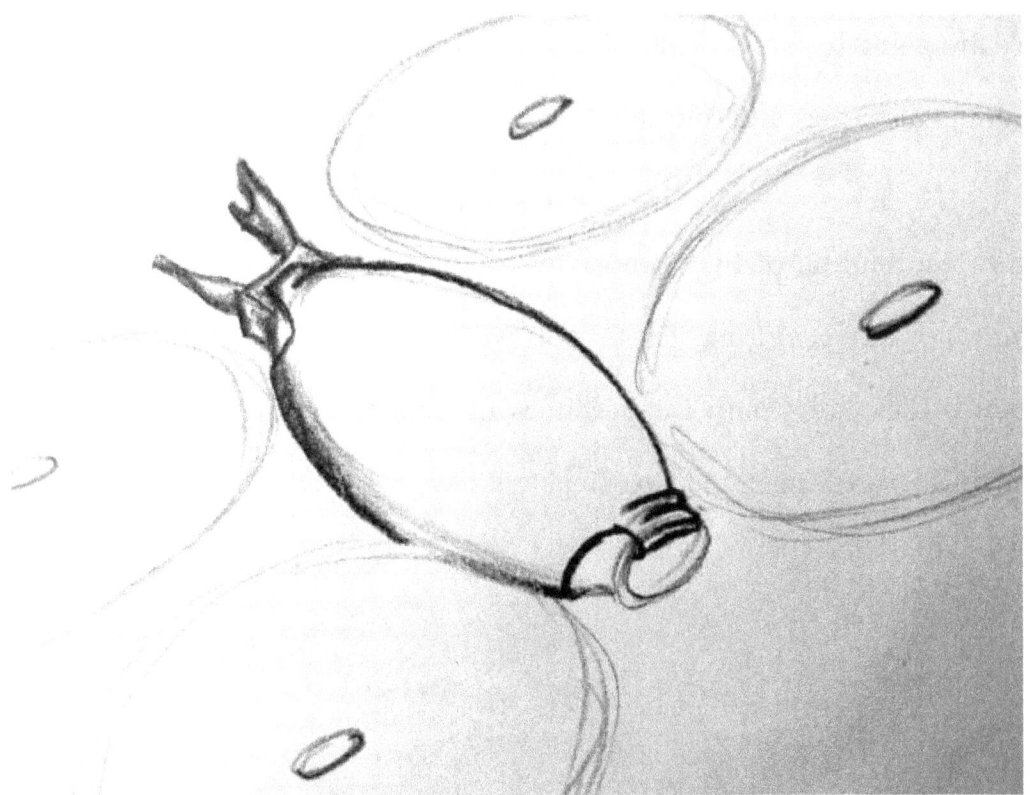

Step 3

Draw a design on top of the body. Give shading in this deign in such a manner that when you are done with hatching and cross hatching, you can scrape out the graphite with a blunt cutter or a butter knife.

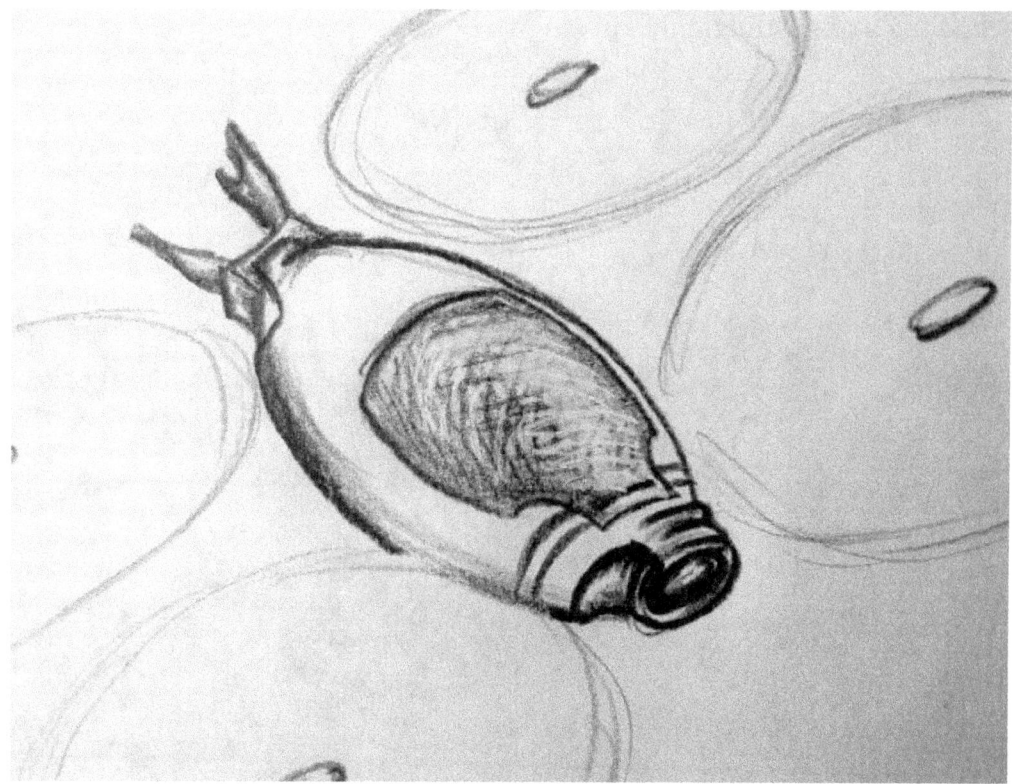

Step 4

Give shading in the remaining part of the upper body which is visible from our perspective. Draw mouth of the airplane's body using concentric ovals. Create depth in the mouth by using variations in shading. Notice that the mouth is joined with the body by a metal fixture and it is given prominence by drawing and shading only.

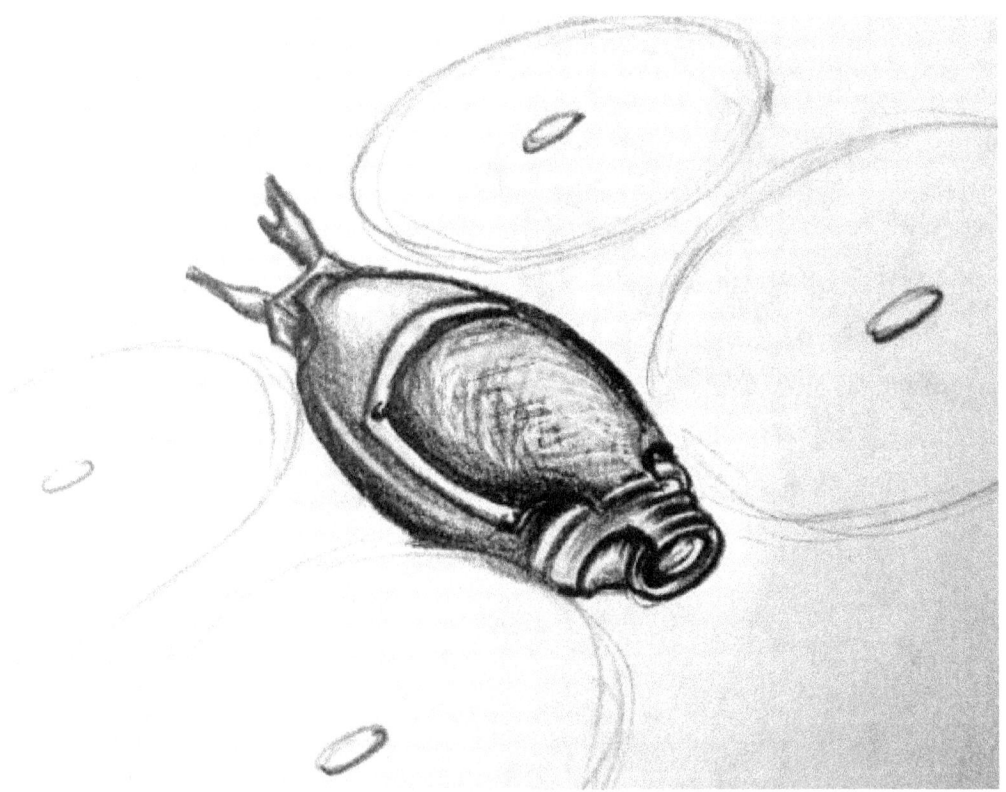

Step 5

Draw the rotor mast in front of the plane, which is joined from the two frontal rings. Give a small circular body in front of this mast.

Draw the joints of four rings with curved metal fixtures and some shafts.

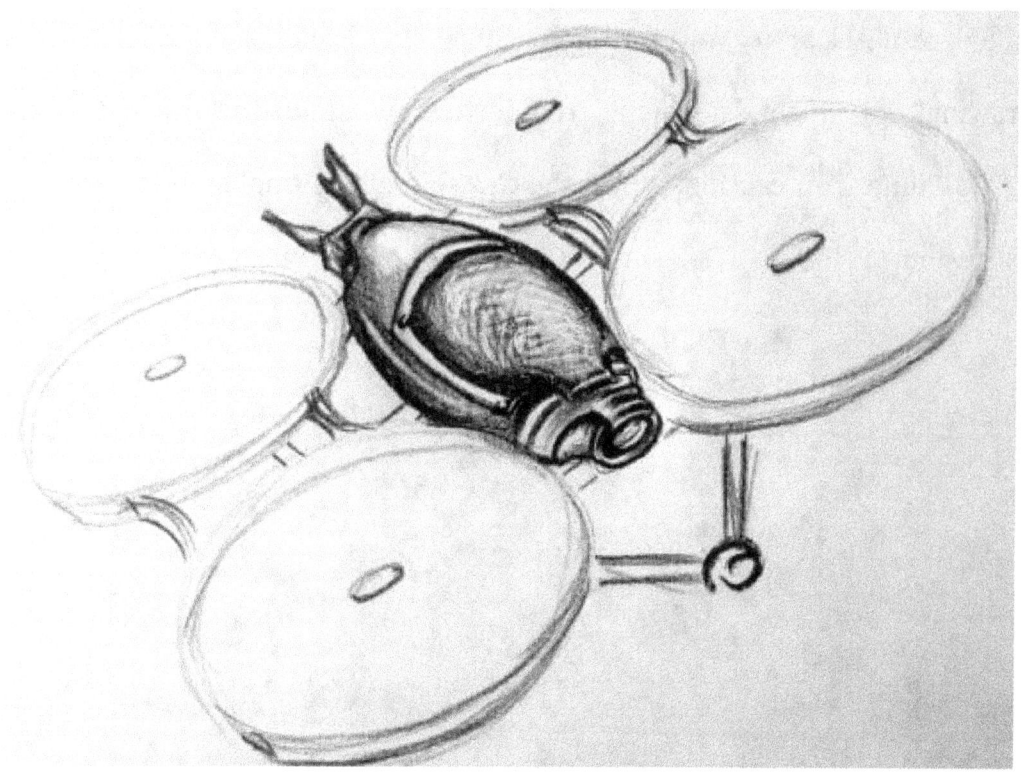

Step 6

Draw frame and rotor blades of the left rings. Give a light drawing so that you can give a final lining later. The blades are joined at the central oval shaped joint, which is also used to draw the remaining frame of the ring.

As you observe and draw each and every part of the rings, the whole drawing will become clear to you gradually. Since this is not a regular object of drawing, you might face some trouble to understand the concept of this Radio Plane. You can look up to the drawing at the final step to avoid any confusion.

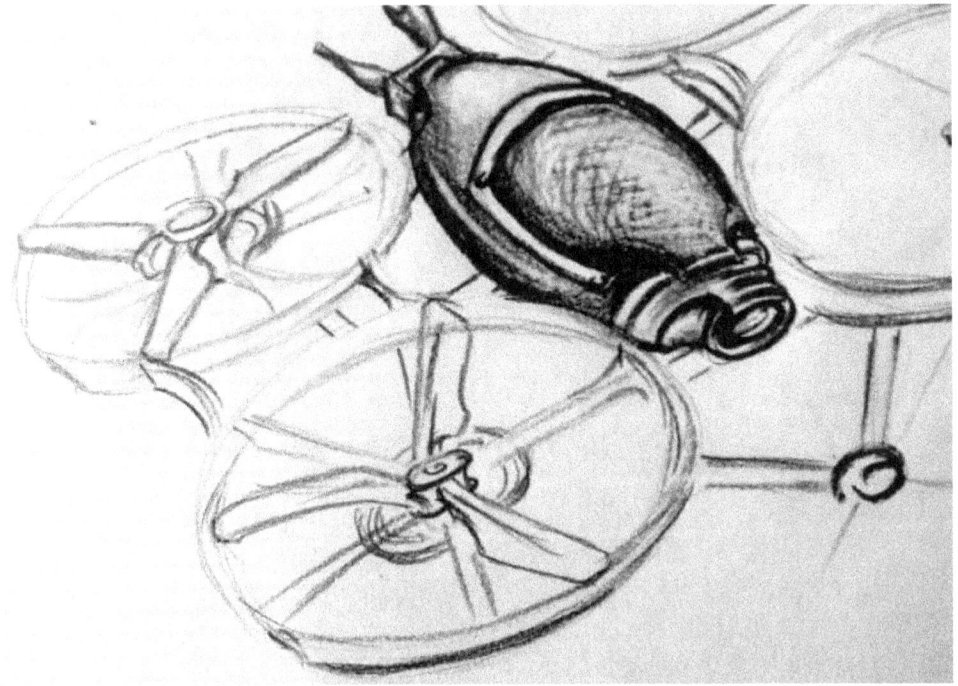

Step 7

Draw the frame and blades for all the rings. Remember to highlight the central oval in each ring.

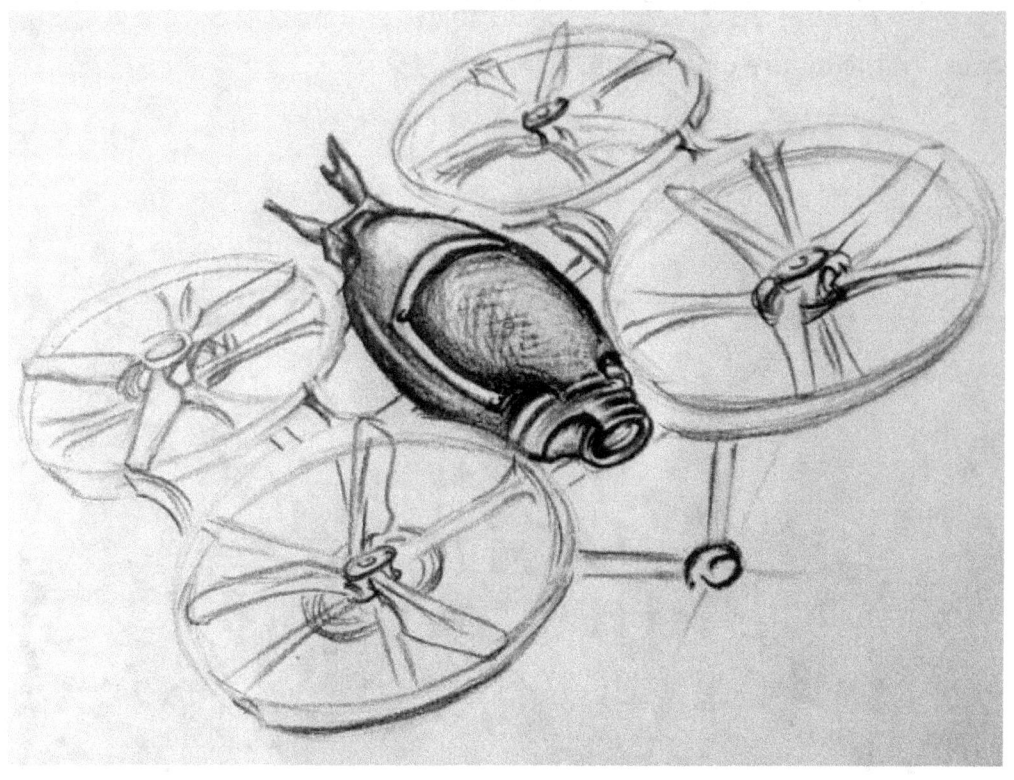

Step 8

Draw a "+" or "x" sign in the central oval to indicate the presence of a bolt. Give final outline and shading in the frame and rotor blades of the rings. The outlines are more dominating in this illustration than the shading because of the nature of drawing.

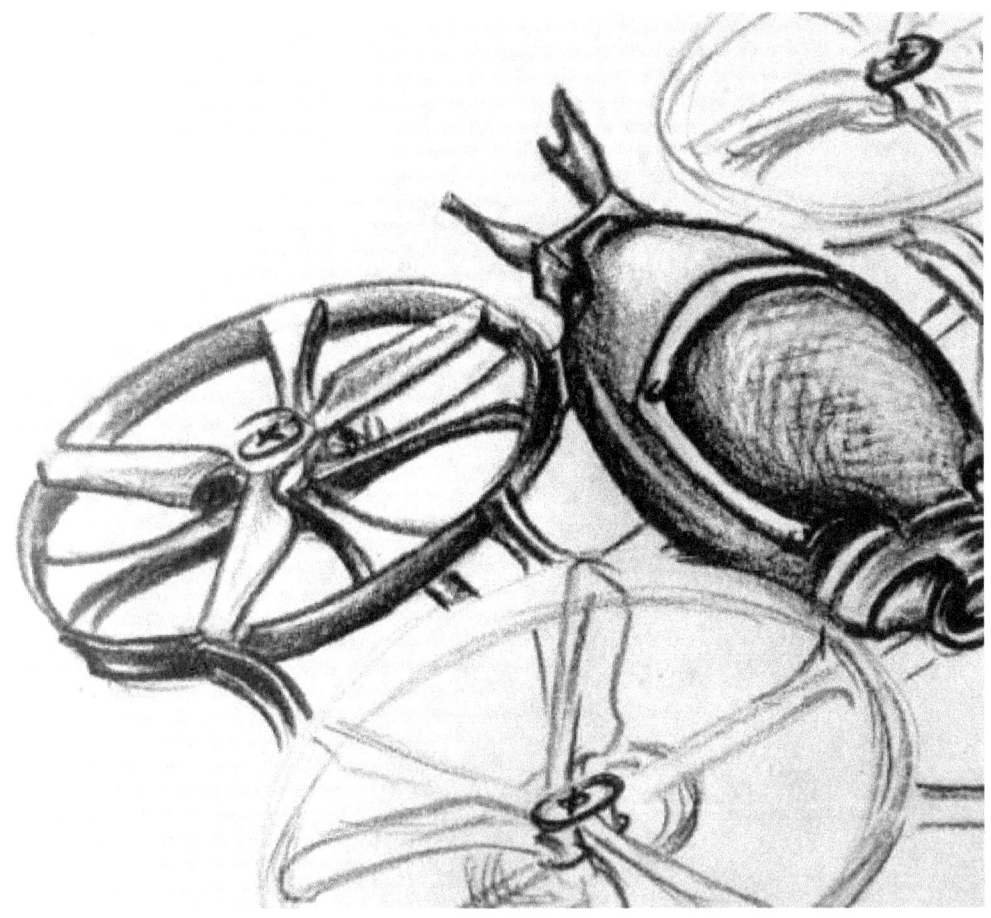

Step 9

The way we gave shading in the hind ring of the Radio Plane in the previous step, give shading in the remaining wings too. Maintaining the style of drawing like that of the previous step, give emphasis on drawing and then on shading.

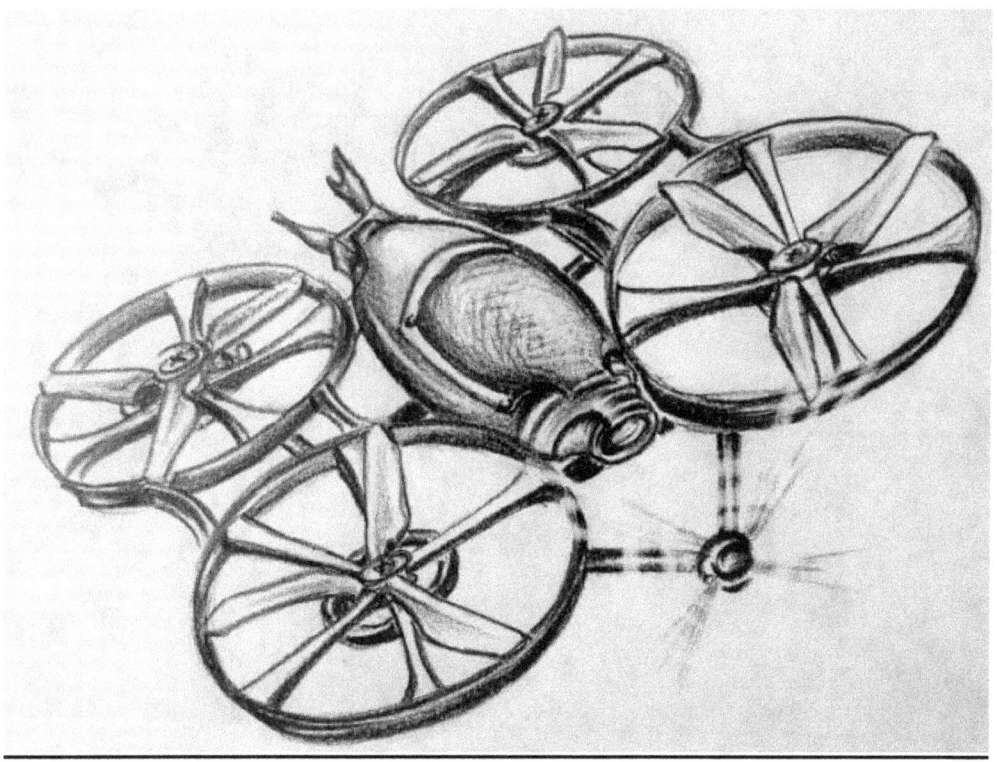

Step 10

To convey movement in the main frontal rotor blades, you have to adopt a trick. Draw straight lines emerging out of the mouth of central rotor mast with a ruler or freehand; as you are comfortable. Then using a sharp eraser, erase a few portions of the straight lines in circular movement. This will create an illusion of movement in the blades.

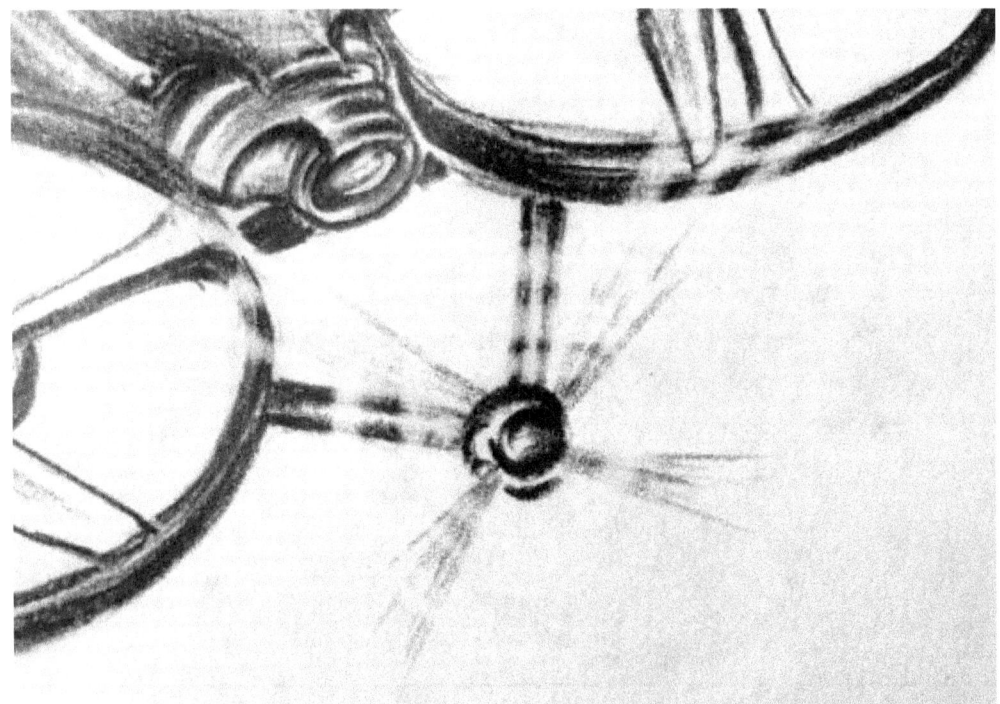

Step 11

Give finishing touches to the shading and drawing of the airplane. The victorian Radio Plane is complete.

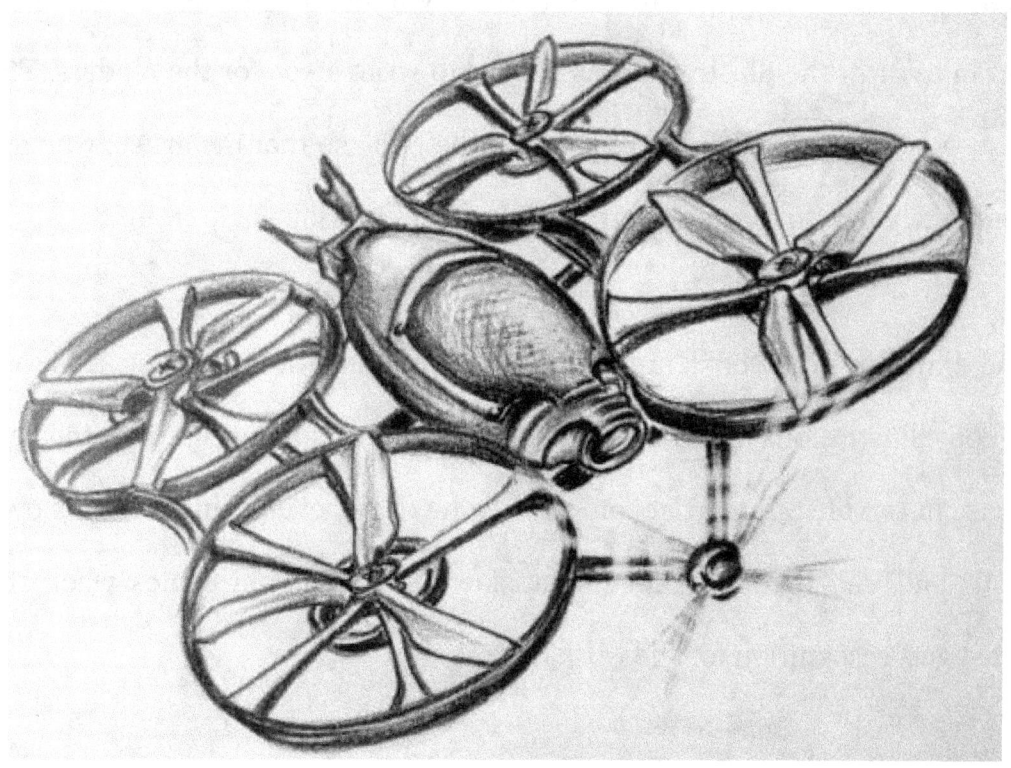

Conclusion

We hope that you enjoyed learning drawing cool drawings from **Cool Stuff Drawing-How to Draw the Best of Cool Drawings in the Easiest Way.** The book is written in a user friendly manner. The best efforts were put in to draw the illustrations as well as to write steps for the readers. The first section was specially introduced in the book so that the artists who are completely new to the genre of pencil drawings can take help from it.

The drawings in the book are a product of creativity of the author. It is easy to copy illustrations from other artists' drawings and paintings. But, the best phase in the life of an artist comes when he draws everything from his own skills and imagination. And the satisfaction of the soul comes when the artist gets recognition for the work he does.

We hope that you achieve the stage of success combined with satisfaction at the earliest. But, it goes unsaid that you need to keep patience for that phase to come. Years of hard work and dedication goes into the success of an artist. We do not intend to discourage you. But, if you have chosen art as your career, you need to have massive patience.

Some artists make solitude as their only friend so that they can give time to their sole creativity and imagination. Sometimes pure imagination does not come when you live with the chores of daily life. Sometimes, you need time with yourself to listen to the call of your soul. If you think that this kind of lifestyle suits you, you can also give it a try to live alone.

Whichever path you chose to become a successful and satiated artist, we wish you all the best.

Thank you!

Thank you for choosing our book, we hope you found it interesting and helpful.

If you liked the book, please give us a favor to write your review.

We would really appreciate this!

If you would like to have a bonus – **FREE BOOK**, please send the screenshot of your review to this e-mail:

kelly.artbooks@gmail.com and we will send you a **FREE BOOK** in PDF as a **GIFT!****

Hope to see you in our future books and good luck in your drawing experience!

** in the e-mail subject please mention the name of the book you reviewed and the author.

www.ingramcontent.com/pod-product-compliance
Lightning Source LLC
Chambersburg PA
CBHW081557170526
45166CB00009B/2729